Cross Purposes

Politics and Culture

James Davison Hunter and John M. Owen IV, Series Editors

The Trouble with History, by Adam Michnik (2014)
Anti-Pluralism, by William A. Galston (2018)
Why Liberalism Failed, by Patrick J. Deneen (2018)
A World Safe for Democracy, by G. John Ikenberry (2020)
The Ecology of Nations, by John M. Owen IV (2023)
Democracy and Solidarity, by James Davison Hunter (2024)
Cross Purposes: Christianity's Broken Bargain with Democracy, by Jonathan
 Rauch (2025)

Cross Purposes

*Christianity's Broken Bargain
with Democracy*

JONATHAN RAUCH

Yale UNIVERSITY PRESS

New Haven and London

Published with the assistance of the Institute for Advanced Studies in Culture, University of Virginia. Also published with assistance from the income of the Frederick John Kingsbury Memorial Fund.

Yale University Press books may be purchased in quantity for educational, business, or promotional use. For information, please e-mail sales.press@yale.edu (U.S. office) or sales@yaleup.co.uk (U.K. office).

Set in Minion type by Integrated Publishing Solutions.
Printed in the United States of America.

Library of Congress Control Number: 2024934534
ISBN 978-0-300-27354-0 (hardcover : alk. paper)

A catalogue record for this book is available from the British Library.

This paper meets the requirements of ANSI/NISO Z39.48-1992 (Permanence of Paper).

10 9 8 7 6 5 4 3 2 1

For Tim Keller and Mark McIntosh
In loving memory

For the Americans the ideas of Christianity and liberty are so completely mingled that it is almost impossible to get them to conceive of the one without the other. . . . In France I had seen the spirits of religion and of freedom almost always marching in opposite directions. In America I found them intimately linked together in joint reign over the same land.

—ALEXIS DE TOCQUEVILLE

Contents

Acknowledgments xi

PROLOGUE. The Dumbest Thing I Ever Wrote 1

ONE. Thin Christianity: Faith's Crisis, Democracy's Peril
*Christianity and democracy are dangerously
out of alignment* 7

TWO. Sharp Christianity: The Church of Fear
*"Flight 93" evangelicalism betrays the church
and the Constitution* 37

THREE. Thick Christianity: The Gospel of Compromise
*There are many ways to reconcile Jesus
with James Madison* 93

EPILOGUE. A Parting Message 138

Notes on Sources 141

Index 149

Acknowledgments

This book originated as a series of lectures at the Institute for Advanced Studies in Culture at the University of Virginia. I am grateful to James Davison Hunter, John Owen, Ty Buckman, and the institute's scholars and staff for their hospitality and guidance.

My work is made possible with the generous support of the Hewlett Foundation, Seth Klarman, Stand Together Trust, and the late and much missed Phil Harvey. The findings, interpretations, and conclusions here are solely my own.

I could not have written this book without the inspiration, instruction, and fellowship of Pastors and Friends. You all know who you are.

Cross Purposes

PROLOGUE
The Dumbest Thing I Ever Wrote

Dear Mark—

In hindsight, there should have been a Neil Simon play about us. Heck, maybe there was.

What an odd couple we were! I, a scrawny Jew from Phoenix; you a tall, broad-shouldered Christian from Chicago. I, a lefty Naderite who railed against the evils of monopolistic corporate power; you, a *National Review* reader who thrilled to the presidential aspirations of George H. W. Bush. (To this day, you are the only person I have ever met in whom Bush Sr. evoked rapturous enthusiasm.)

But we did have something in common. On our college housing forms that summer, we had both checked "classical" under "music preference." That was enough to bring us together as freshman roommates.

Even so, I found a way to be contentious. You rooted for your hometown team—the Chicago Symphony and its famous conductor, Sir Georg Solti. I was no fan of Maestro Solti, whom I nicknamed the Hungarian Butcher. Even worse, I complained that the vaunted Chicago brass played too loud. It's a wonder we didn't come to blows.

Then there was that other difference. The Big Difference.

You were what in those days certain students called, very unkindly, God Squad. (Prejudice against religion is nothing new, on campus or off.) You attended church services on Sundays while I slept in. You not only talked the talk, you walked the walk. I tried to be respectful of you as a person but didn't hide my lack of respect for the Christian religion. Not yet out of my teens, I was what was known as a militant atheist, a confrontational unbeliever.

I had my reasons. From age five or so, I had known that I was different from other boys because I felt magnetically attracted to handsome boys and muscular men. Though I would not find a name for my obsession until age 25, I knew that Christianity was hostile to someone like me. One reason I denied the truth about myself for so long was the discrimination I feared from Christians who relied on the authority of the Bible to hate me. In my youth, I could not spin the AM radio dial on a Sunday morning without hearing some preacher denounce the sinfulness, decadence, and danger of homosexuality. Christianity did not seem very compassionate to me.

I was different in another way, too. In second grade, I began seven years of Hebrew school—after-school religious classes— two or three days a week, and I attended Jewish sleepaway camp every summer. My parents were not pious but thought I should know my tradition. I was bar mitzvahed and knew the prayers. Yet early on, I knew I did not believe in God, *could* not believe in God. I can't tell you how I knew; I just *knew* that the idea of a big father in the sky who creates the entire universe yet attends minutely to man's everyday affairs makes no sense, and that the tales in the Bible could not possibly be true to life. If the tales *were* true, they showed God and his followers doing some rotten and senseless things. For a time, in camp the summer before high school, I tried believing. I donned tefillin twice a day, said the brachot, and tried to fit in. When that had no effect, I gave up on faith (though not on Judaism; that identity is written in my blood).

By the time we met, I believed the world would be better off without religion—especially Christianity. I saw the church as cruel and hypocritical and had arrived at college armed to argue the point. I had imbibed the writings of Bertrand Russell. Though "Why I Am Not a Christian" was his most famous anti-religious essay, my personal favorite was "Has Religion Made Useful Contributions to Civilization?" (The answer: "It helped in early days to fix the calendar, and it caused Egyptian priests to chronicle eclipses with such care that in time they became able to predict them. These two services I am prepared to acknowledge, but I do not know of any others.")

So that was the moment when Destiny, in the form of the university housing office, threw us together. I was prepared to confront Christianity, but I was not prepared for *you*. Within the first couple of weeks, I realized you were . . . different.

You did not proselytize but shone by example, exhibiting gentleness and courtesy to all you met. Unlike many of the Christians I had heard preaching and posturing on the radio, you seemed confident and secure in your faith. When I teased or goaded you, you would chuckle, not bristle. Though your politics were conservative—you were a devoted participant in the campus Conservative Party—you never let politics preempt kindness. Once, when a gay rights petition circulated on campus, you were among the first to sign, saying it was God's place, not yours, to judge. You treated me with forbearance (what I would later recognize as *grace*) and did the same for others. Much later, years after you had taken degrees at Yale and Oxford and General Theological Seminary, ascended to the Anglican priesthood, become the Reverend Dr. Mark A. McIntosh, and authored more books on theology and Christian mysticism than I could count, one of your former classmates recalled that even in your seminary days you had had a mystical aura. Looking back, I see I had picked up on that.

You were not a saint, to be sure. But you were something the 18-year-old version of me found oxymoronic: a good Christian.

I didn't convert. I didn't change my mind. You were the portal, though, to a change of heart. Once I had seen what Christianity could be, it became a subject of curiosity for me, instead of contempt—something I had to know more about. I imagined that one day I might even write about it.

Later in life, with your example before me, I came to cherish close Christian friends, some of them—such as the late Pastor Tim Keller, the co-dedicatee of this book—among the wisest and deepest people I have known. I came to see that the confrontational, contemptuous style of my youthful atheism, and later of the so-called New Atheists, had it backwards. Yes, religion can be stupid; but people make religion stupid, not the other way around.

In the years after our student days, my politics evolved in your direction. Ralph Nader and Bertrand Russell were replaced in my pantheon by John Locke and James Madison, William James and C. S. Peirce, George Orwell and Karl Popper. My view of spirituality evolved, too. I came to see that people who believe in God have an ability I lack. They receive frequencies I can't detect, which give their worlds a dimensionality, a layer of meaning, that my world lacks. This does not make their view—*your* view—better or truer than mine. But I am not defensive about likening my atheism to color blindness, because faith is a part of the human experience in which I do not share.

My career in journalism led me deeply into politics and government. For a long time, I barely gave religion a thought. It seemed to have receded into the background of American life, except when the latest priestly or pastoral scandal flamed into view. Newspapers didn't cover religion much, except in the Sunday church pages which no one I knew read.

When I did dip into religion, my view was superficial. In 2003, for *The Atlantic*, I joyfully celebrated what I called *apatheism*, which I defined as not caring very much one way or the other about religion. Because religion is a source of social divisiveness and volatility, I predicted that apatheism would tone down friction and represented "nothing less than a major civilizational advance." It was, I gloated, "the product of a determined cultural effort to discipline the religious mindset, and often of an equally determined personal effort to master the spiritual passions. It is not a lapse. It is an achievement."

Ahem. Let's just say that's not how things turned out. Instead we live in a society which, on both left and right, has imported religious zeal into secular politics and exported politics into religion, bringing partisan polarization and animosity to levels unseen since the Civil War.

That crisis is the subject of this book. The first chapter concerns what I call *Thin Christianity*. The question it asks is: why should secular Americans, including many who feel they have a beef with organized religion, care about the state of Christian America? To put it another way: what happens to our liberal democracy if American Christianity is no longer able, or no longer willing, to perform the functions on which our constitutional order depends? The alarming answer is that the crisis for Christianity has turned out to be a crisis for democracy.

The second chapter takes up *Sharp Christianity*. The question it turns to is: what happens to American liberal democracy when a prevalent strain of Christianity becomes not only secularized but politicized, partisan, confrontational, and divisive? The answer: the liberalism on which both the Constitution and modern American Christianity depend is gravely

weakened, setting off a dangerous spiral of mutual degrada-
tion. In contradistinction with so-called post-liberals, I maintain that American Protestantism's current crisis is the fault
not primarily of a hostile secular world, but of tragic decisions
made by Christians themselves.

The third chapter considers an alternative path, which I
call *Thick Christianity*. Is it possible, despite what's alleged by
both Christian critics of liberal democracy and secular critics
of Christianity, for Christianity to align itself with constitutional pluralism—not just strategically, but theologically and
spiritually? Can we envision a rapprochement rooted in the
deepest traditions and teachings of Jesus? For a hopeful answer, we will look, perhaps unexpectedly, to the Church of Jesus
Christ of Latter-day Saints; and then consider the prospects for
a new entente which honors both Jesus and James Madison.

So, Mark, please accept this book as penitence for the
dumbest thing I ever wrote—and maybe also for the dumb
things I said to you. I hope, in these pages, to be part of the
solution at a moment when American Christianity is in crisis,
and when its crisis is mine, too.

1

Thin Christianity

Faith's Crisis, Democracy's Peril

Christianity and democracy are dangerously out of alignment

Some Americans may recall when a leading public figure impiously claimed to rival Jesus's fame. No, not Donald Trump, though he did do that. This was in 1966, when John Lennon, a member of the Beatles, told a journalist, "Christianity will go. It will vanish and shrink. I needn't argue about that; I know I'm right and I will be proved right. We're more popular than Jesus now. I don't know which will go first—rock and roll or Christianity."

The remark was first published in London's *Evening Standard* without incident. But when it was reprinted in an American teen magazine, Tommy Charles, a talk-show host with Alabama's WAQY Radio (pronounced "wacky radio"), seized upon it. He launched an impromptu "Ban the Beatles" campaign, which took off, igniting record-burnings, outraged sermons, a denunciation by the Pope, and death threats against the Beatles from the likes of the KKK. As the band scrambled to save bookings, Lennon went before the press to apologize, which calmed things down. Still, fears for the band's safety, exacerbated by a scare when an explosion disrupted a concert (it

turned out to be a cherry bomb), contributed to their decision
to stop touring.

The Beatles are still popular. So is Jesus. In the decade
following Lennon's remark, evangelicalism experienced a resurgence, becoming the culturally dominant strain of Christianity in the United States.

The burden of this book, however, is that Lennon was not
entirely wrong. Something *has* happened to American Christianity—something which has made it less able, less willing,
or less able *and* less willing to support the liberal democracy
of which it is part. This change, as more than a few Christians
argue, has become a crisis for American Christianity. It is also
a crisis for American democracy.

The Great Dechurching

Crisis? Consider the facts. While not "vanished," Christianity
has certainly shrunk. Barna Group, an independent research
organization, reports that only 25 percent of Americans are "prac-
ticing Christians" (as defined by self-identification, church
attendance, and prioritizing faith), down by almost half since
2000. Gallup reports that in 2021, U.S. church membership fell
below 50 percent for the first time. Over the past twenty-five
years, "about 40 million adults in America today used to go to
church but no longer do, which accounts for around 16 percent of our adult population," write Jim Davis and Michael
Graham in their 2023 book *The Great Dechurching: Who's Leaving, Why Are They Going, and What Will It Take to Bring Them
Back?* They note that almost half of Americans attend church
less than once a year, versus 17 percent in 1972. Given that most
social trends happen fairly slowly, the rate at which the United
States is dechurching is startling. According to the Pew Re-

search Center, one of the country's preeminent polling organizations, the percentage identifying as Christian fell by 15 percentage points between 2007 and 2021—about a percent a year. "This is not a gradual shift," write Davis and Graham; "it is a jolting one."

Churches, too, are caving in—especially smaller ones. Davis and Graham write that at least 86 close (on net) every week. Research by Faith Communities Today, reported in *Twenty Years of Congregational Change: The 2020 Faith Communities Today Overview,* finds that the average church congregation shrank from 137 members at the turn of the century to less than half of that by 2020—a decline so great that their ability to maintain basic programs is in doubt. The sociologist Scott Thumma has predicted that the country will lose 30 to 40 percent of its congregations in the next 20 years.

I could spend the rest of this chapter reeling off similar statistics. John Lennon, call your office.

Within that trend is nested another. For some time, it appeared that Christian devotional energy was shifting away from moderate ecumenical denominations while white evangelical churches thrived, but that is no longer true.* According to the Pew Religion and Public Life Survey and the Public Religion Research Institute, the number of white evangelicals in the United States has declined from almost a fourth of the population in 2006 to barely more than an eighth in 2022—the

* How to define evangelicalism—theologically, culturally, politically, or all three—is a contested question which I will not try to tackle here. Like many pollsters and scholars, I assume people are evangelical if they say they are. Evangelical identifiers include, among others, many Southern Baptists, Pentecostals, members of the Presbyterian Church in America, and members of nondenominational churches.

year when their numbers dropped *below* those of white main-line Protestants. In a panel discussion hosted by Religion News Service in 2022, Bob Smietana, a national reporter for that organization and the author of the 2022 book *Reorganized Religion: The Reshaping of the American Church and Why It Matters,* said, "There used to be this idea that conservative churches would grow and liberal churches would shrink. Well, now they're *all* shrinking. Especially if you're mostly white."

Meanwhile, the share of Americans professing to participate in "no religion" has increased at eye-watering speed. According to Gallup polling, the percentage of "nones," the religiously unaffiliated, was in the 3 percent range from 1948 to 1970; rose but remained below 10 percent from 1971 to 2001; and then skyrocketed to above 20 percent by 2021. "Nones" now account for as large a share of the population as all white Protestants combined. The percentage of Americans saying religion is "very important" to them declined from 62 percent in 1998 to only 39 percent in 2023, according to polling by the *Wall Street Journal* and the University of Chicago's NORC research center.

Christianity is not about to disappear, nor will it cease being America's predominant religious tradition; John Lennon was not *that* right. Many of those who stop attending church or disaffiliate with it remain under its influence. In his book *Nonverts: The Making of Ex-Christian America,* Stephen Bullivant notes that "an *ex*-Christian nation is not simply the same as a *non*-Christian one. A culture that used to be Christian, just like a person who used to be one, carries much of the past along with it."

Yet even that muscle memory of Christianity will fade as more children and grandchildren of "nones" grow up without inherited knowledge of Christianity. So far, generational succession has driven unswervingly toward disaffiliation. "Nones" skew young: two-thirds of them are aged 18 to 44, according to Bullivant. In 2022, Pew found that only about half of Americans in their twenties identified as Christian, versus three-fourths or more of people in their mid-fifties and older. Statistics like those led the Public Religion Research Institute's Robert P. Jones to write, in his 2016 book *The End of White Christian America,* "These numbers point to one undeniable conclusion: white Protestant Christians—both mainline and evangelical—are aging and quickly losing ground as a proportion of the population." His conclusion: "White Christian America's heyday has passed."

Within those declining totals are other signs of distress. According to Barna, in 2022, 42 percent of pastors said they had considered quitting in the past year—an increase of nine percentage points over a year earlier. Stress, loneliness, and "current political divisions" were the top three reasons. My own conversations with pastors suggest that Barna's figure is very plausible. One pastor told me he had almost quit four times in the past few years. Referring to parishioners who bring the culture wars with them to church, he said, "These guys are a special kind of relentless." Pastors complain—so often that it has become a mantra—that they get their congregants for two hours a week, whereas cable news gets them for twelve.

The term *crisis* does not seem exaggerated.

Nietzsche's Prophecy

Today, a group of so-called "post-liberals"—led by religious conservatives such as Sohrab Ahmari, Patrick Deneen, Yoram Hazony, and Adrian Vermeule—look at the crisis of Christianity and know just what to blame: liberalism.

I should pause to clarify how I mean *liberalism,* here and throughout these pages. I don't mean the center-left progressivism which the term often signifies in contemporary American politics ("George McGovern was a liberal Democrat"). I mean the modern tradition of freedom, toleration, minority rights, and the rule of law on which the American republic was founded. Some people use the term *classical liberalism,* but I want to indicate something even broader: the tradition, dating back to the seventeenth century, which grounds *ethics* in the proposition that all humans are created free and equal; *politics* in the proposition that the people are sovereign and government's powers are limited and consensual; and *authority* in the proposition that everyone follows the same rules and enjoys the same rights. Liberal regimes regard individuals, not groups, as the fundamental bearers of rights and responsibilities. To make public decisions when differences arise, they deploy public debate and open-ended, decentralized, rules-based processes.

Modern liberal societies rely on three linked social systems: liberal democracy to make political choices; market capitalism to make economic choices; and science and other forms of open critical exchange to make epistemic choices (that is, decisions about truth and knowledge). A hallmark of liberal social systems is that the same rules apply to all, regardless of identity or tribe. In principle, anyone can vote in an election, trade in a market, or replicate an experiment. For liberals, the answer to the question "Who's in charge here?" should normally be: *no one in particular.* Although liberal regimes have often failed to live up to their ideals, they have generally improved over time. And by transcending tribe, renouncing authoritarianism, and substituting rules for rulers, liberal social orders can coordinate human activity among hundreds of millions of strangers, across nations and continents, without central control or direction—something no other social system can do.

In secular liberalism, however, post-liberals see something darker: an aggressively godless, consumerist, hyper-individualistic, and self-absorbed culture which dissolves faith and tradition—inherently, not just incidentally. In Chapter 2, I will explain why I think they are wrong. If Christians want to know why they are losing adherents and influence, they should look in the mirror. Yet there are important grains of truth in the post-liberal perspective. To give it its due, we can reach back to the most scathing and influential critic of both Christianity *and* secular liberalism, the prophet who imagined more than a century ago where we might seem to be today.

Just to lay my cards on the table, I should confess that I regard Friedrich Nietzsche with distaste. I find little by way of coherence in his works and nothing by way of empirical rigor. His generalizations are wild, his hyperbole reckless, his contradictions rampant, and his elitism noxious. Yet the almost hallucinatory power of his rhetoric and his genius for the startling aperçu reach across 150 years and grab our throats. And where secular liberalism is concerned, he did see it coming.

Unlike today's post-liberals, Nietzsche is hostile to both religion and traditional morals. He makes no bones about his contempt for Christian teaching, which he believes sanctifies shame, conformism, mediocrity, passivity, and other attributes which stunt ambition, creativity, and achievement. "Christianity . . . crushed and shattered man completely," he writes in *Human, All Too Human.* "Assuming that he believes at all, the everyday Christian is a pitiful figure, a man who really cannot count up to three, and who besides, precisely because of his mental incompetence, would not deserve such a punishment as Christianity promises him."* If Nietzsche were running a modern ad campaign, he might borrow the U.S. Army's slo-

* *Human, All Too Human: A Book for Free Spirits,* trans. Marion Faber with Stephen Lehmann (University of Nebraska Press, 1984), 85 and 86.

gan: *Be all you can be!* We must rise to the heights of our potential, find greatness and follow where it leads, or at least the
greatest of us must reach those heights. To do so, we must shed
the vulgar servility and bovine stupefaction which Christianity inculcates.

And yet . . . Nietzsche acknowledges that Christianity,
while morally disfiguring and "arising from an *error,*" does provide a source of values, something which secularism is hard put
to do. "When religious ideas are destroyed one is troubled by
an uncomfortable emptiness and deprivation," he writes in *The
Gay Science.* "Christianity, it seems to me, is still needed by
most people in old Europe even today."

Or rather, Christianity *did* provide a source of values; but
today, he famously declares, God is dead, "and we have killed
him." By "we" he means the modern secular order and ideas
like liberalism and Marxism, which undercut the authority and
enchantment of religion. He regards deicide as a seminal event,
a turning point in human development ("there has never been
a greater deed"), because while Christianity's decline may leave
ordinary people adrift and aimless, it clears space for a bold,
visionary few—of whom Nietzsche is himself the exemplar.
These gifted moral visionaries are able to rise above bourgeois
conformism, create their own moral frames, and share those
frames with humanity, such that "whoever is born after us . . .
will belong to a higher history than all history hitherto."*

To my modern liberal eye, this is self-aggrandizing and
sophomoric rubbish, and reckless to boot. Although Nietzsche
did not propound a politics, one readily sees how his teachings
open the door to political illiberalism and even the outright
fascism of, for example, his sister, an ardent Nazi. His slogan-

---

* *The Gay Science,* trans. Walter Kaufmann (Random House, 1974), at Nos.
196, 287, and 181.

eering about supermen and slave morality and the death of god was tailor-made to be twisted into a political program of domination and a morality of might-makes-right.

Still, one must acknowledge merit in Nietzsche's diagnosis. In today's America, we see evidence everywhere of the inadequacy of secular liberalism to provide meaning, exaltation, spirituality, transcendence, and morality anchored in more than the self. As America has secularized over the past 50 years, cynicism about politics, disdain for institutions, and discontent with public life have risen. The aforementioned *WSJ*/NORC survey showed that as the percentage of Americans saying religion is very important to them has declined, so have the percentages of those characterizing patriotism, community involvement, and having children as very important. What value tested by the pollsters *rose* in importance over the period? Just one: "Making money."

Alt-Religion

Unlike the conservative post-liberals, I find much to celebrate in twenty-first-century America's values. Back when I celebrated "apatheism," I supposed that as organized religious participation declined, Americans might find other sources of values, perhaps better ones. And to a remarkable extent, they have done so. As a homosexual American, I owe my marriage—and the astonishing liberation I have enjoyed during my lifetime— to the advance of enlightened secular values. None of what I am about to say is intended to negate the very real social and moral progress which secular culture has achieved—or to deny the long record of religiously inspired cruelty and bigotry. I am not on board with those who hanker for a time when "morality," "faith," and "tradition" gave cover to oppression, superstition, and dogma.

That said, it has become pretty evident that secularism has not been able to fill what has been called the "God-shaped hole" in American life. Because the quest for spirituality and meaning is deeply human, it is insistent. We need commitments to something larger than ourselves, communities rooted in more than transactional gains, truths which transcend time and place, and missions worth sacrificing for; and if we do not find them in institutionalized religion, we will look elsewhere. In her 2020 book *Strange Rites: New Religions for a Godless World,* Tara Isabella Burton catalogs some of the secular movements which have arisen as vehicles for spiritual fervor: wellness culture, occultism, wicca, radical social justice ("wokeness"), the New Age, techno-utopianism, the alt-right, and more. Q-Anon, MAGA's cultic cousin, comes complete with its own prophet, eschatology, and redemptive mission—all twisted into a grimacing, politicized caricature of religion. On the other side of the ideological spectrum, many observers have noticed the quasi-religious nature of wokeness. The linguist John McWhorter even rejects the "quasi": "I do not mean that these people's ideology is 'like' a religion," he writes in *Woke Racism: How a New Religion Has Betrayed Black America;* "I mean that it actually *is* a religion. An anthropologist would see no difference in type between Pentecostalism and this new form of antiracism."

These "bespoke religions," as Burton calls them, are invested with spiritual and moral significance, but they lack institutional bases and theological anchors, and their adherents "reject authority, institution, creed, and moral universalism. They value intuition, personal feeling, and experiences. They demand to rewrite their own scripts." She adds that "much of the responsibility for that shift belongs to [religious] institutions themselves. Traditional religions, traditional political hierarchies, and traditional understandings of society have been unwilling or unable to offer compellingly meaningful accounts of the world, provide their members with purpose, foster sustainable communities, or put forth evocative rituals."

Secular movements have their benefits; I am not here to condemn them. But it turns out that none of them is capable of replacing the great religions where anchoring moral codes, maintaining durable communities, and transmitting values are concerned. As Jessica Grose wrote in the *New York Times* in 2023, paraphrasing the sociologist Phil Zuckerman, "A soccer team can't provide spiritual solace in the face of death, it probably doesn't have a weekly charitable call and there's no sense of connection to a heritage that goes back generations."

Secular pseudo-religions also do not seem to replicate the positive effects of the real thing. "Social scientists have produced a mountain of evidence that religion is good for you," write John Micklethwait and Adrian Wooldridge in their 2009 book *God Is Back: How the Global Revival of Faith Is Changing the World.* Organized religious participation correlates with greater happiness and well-being, longer life, stronger immune systems and lower blood pressure, lower crime and drug use, and greater civic engagement. Most people cannot reap the same benefits at home. "It is the communal forms of religious participation, rather than merely private practices, that most powerfully affect health," notes Tyler J. VanderWeele of Harvard's School of Public Health. Other research suggests that the decline of religious participation may be an important factor in the alarming rise in the United States of deaths of despair.

It turns out that Nietzsche was right: love religion or hate it, its communal functions are very hard to replace. Where he went wrong was in assuming that self-actualization and self-elevation could substitute for religion, even among elites. A

country of 350 million would-be *Übermenschen* cannot thrive.
And so, writes Brink Lindsey, of the Niskanen Center, in his
Substack blog, *The Permanent Problem,*

> the sunny view of organized religion's retreat as human-
> ity's intellectual advance really can't be sustained. We are
> not seeing the decline of supernaturalism so much as its
> privatization or atomization. Belief in the fantastic has
> escaped from its traditional repositories, where it served
> to bind us into communities founded on a shared sense
> of the sacred, and now exists as a disconnected jumble,
> accessible as a purely individual consumer choice to guide
> one's personal search for meaning. What the sociologist
> Peter Berger called the "sacred canopy" has shattered and
> fallen to earth; we pick up shards here or there, on our
> own or in small groups, and whatever we manage to build
> with them is necessarily more fleeting and less inclusive
> than what we experienced before.

What My Younger Self Missed

What did I get wrong, then, in my "apatheistic" past? My
younger self acknowledged the social benefits of religious participation but imagined that other institutions and pursuits
could substitute, an assumption which proved wrong as an
empirical matter.

My younger self also took the stability of both democracy and Christianity too much for granted. Like many of us
in the aftermath of the Cold War, I was too ready to indulge in
liberal-democratic triumphalism, forgetting how hard it is to
build and maintain the value structures which support democracy. We have since learned, painfully, what any Iraqi or Af-
ghan can tell you: air-dropping elections and constitutions on

a morally unprepared society does not work. At the same time, I didn't foresee the extent to which mainline Protestantism would collapse as a source of public values, and I certainly didn't foresee the extent to which evangelical Protestantism would turn resentful, confrontational, and authoritarian.

In hindsight, too, I did not appreciate the implicit bargain between American democracy and American Christianity. I would have said that the basic deal was to leave each other alone—"wall of separation" and all that. Their only bargain, I thought, was to make no bargain; to the greatest extent possible, religion and government should tend to their separate businesses and not interfere with each other.

Although there is much merit in mutual non-intervention, I should have paid more attention to the American Founders who, while opposing the admixture of religion with government, warned that republicanism would rely in part on religious underpinnings. John Adams, for instance, famously wrote: "We have no government armed with power capable of contending with human passions unbridled by morality and religion. Avarice, ambition, revenge, or gallantry would break the strongest cords of our Constitution as a whale goes through a net. Our Constitution was made only for a moral and religious people. It is wholly inadequate to the government of any other." Adams was more of a virtuecrat than some of the other Founders, but even the freethinker Thomas Jefferson said he considered "ethics, *as well as religion,* as supplements to law in the government of man" (my italics).

The Founders did not expect Christianity or any other religion to have greater loyalty to the Constitution than to God. They famously rejected the establishment of a state religion or any other explicit state-church alliance, believing that entanglement would harm both parties. Religion's job is not to *support* republican government. They did, however, generally believe that religion—Christianity, for all intents and purposes—was important for *stabilizing* republican government, because it teaches virtue and thereby makes Americans more governable. In his 2007 book *Christianity and American Democracy,* Hugh Heclo summarizes the view of early America's greatest observer, Alexis de Tocqueville:

> Tocqueville has no doubt that the tendency of democracy to unleash passions for physical pleasure, to push individuals toward a short-sighted, brutish materialism, is fully on display in America. His claim is that it is therefore all the more important that religious beliefs counter these democratic tendencies by drawing attention to man's immortal soul and elevating his affections and mere natural reason toward what is majestic, pure, and eternal. Without the active presence of spiritual conceptions in society—the recognition that an integral part of each person is implicated in realities beyond this material world— human beings in the democratic age are in great danger of becoming degraded into something less than fully human.

By the same token, the Founders did not believe that only the religious (or only Christians) can be good citizens in a republic, or that the government must be Christian formally or in its character. Nor were they naïve about religion's purity or reliability; like other contending factions, churches can be self-serving and need to be restrained by proper institutional arrangements. As Adams warned, "Religion, superstition, oaths, education, laws, all give way before passions, interest, and power, which can be resisted only by passions, interest, and power." Rather, the Founders were making the same point the conservative thinker George F. Will made in 1984 in his classic book

Statecraft as Soulcraft: the businesses of making public laws and shaping public morals are inevitably interwoven, implying that politics and religion cannot simply be strangers to one another, even if they try—which they shouldn't.

In the modern United States, however, the consensus among liberals has moved toward further separation—cultural as well as formal—between church and state. And, yes, very often democracy and Christianity *should* leave each other alone. The greater danger lies in too much entanglement, not too little. It is neither necessary nor desirable for church and state to be *allied;* at least in the American context, blurring their separate responsibilities would compromise their independence, legitimacy, and effectiveness. In the United States, a state religion is a bad idea, as are efforts to write religious observance (Sabbath closings, for example) into law.

Even so, Tocqueville and the Founders were not wrong: it is important for Christianity and democracy to be reasonably well *aligned.* Neither can thrive if they are at cross purposes. I did not fully appreciate that in 2003, and I think too few Americans on both sides of the line, secular and religious, appreciate it today.

Four Existential Questions

Now I wish to make a stronger claim. It is a claim I would have vehemently rejected in my youth, but one which I owe to my regular and deep engagement these past few years with friends in the religious world. My claim is not just that secular liberalism and religious faith are *instrumentally* interdependent but that each is *intrinsically* reliant on the other to build a morally and epistemically complete and coherent account of the world. In other words, the structure of the moral and epistemic universes is such that both ways of thought are incomplete *even in principle.* Although they are always in tension and sometimes in outright conflict, neither by itself will ever be able to satisfy human needs to cope with the world.

I believe there are four questions to which most individuals seek answers in order to feel complete as moral beings. Most people also feel more comfortable belonging to groups which furnish or at least encourage *shared* answers. Of course, there are other important questions, too; the four I have in mind are not all-encompassing; nor do most people go around worrying about them while getting the kids to school or fixing the car. But all of them require some kind of social account if we are to believe we live in a morally coherent world; and all of them concern us individually to some degree, even if we rarely sit down and cogitate about them. As a handy mnemonic, I think of them as four M's.

> *Mortality.* How can life have meaning if all it leads to, ultimately, is death?
> *Morality.* What is the ultimate basis for belief in, and understanding of, right and wrong?
> *Murder.* Why is the world so full of suffering, injustice, and violence?
> *Miracles.* How can we explain the world without recourse to magic—thus reliably, systematically, and adjudicably?

Again, I do not claim that each of these questions preoccupies every individual. By temperament, some people think about them a lot, others not at all; some are bothered by one question but not another. Personally, I have never had a problem with mortality. Since childhood, I have felt quite content believing I am a soulless clump of cells which will self-destruct.

Philosophers and societies, however, cannot shirk the four M's; of necessity, they have struggled with them for millennia. The reason I raise them in the present context—the existential interdependence of secularism and spirituality—is that secularism can cope with only two of them, and spiritualism only with the other two.

Mortality and Morality

We cope with the fact of death by pushing it to the background of everyday life, yet it remains existentially terrifying—not just because of the physical reality of death but also because of the nihilism it implies. Death seems to negate all human accomplishment, all meaning. If we come to nothing in the end, why does anything we do matter? Why devote ourselves to the next generation? Why even bother getting through the day? Purely secular thinking can explain how humans evolved, how we fit in with the (much) larger universe, and how we differ from other creatures. Perhaps someday it will explain the mysteries of consciousness and selfhood. But it cannot give us a reason for being here or explain why we are worth caring about, or why (or even whether) a human life matters more than any other cluster of chemically active molecules. In his 2023 book *Facing Death: Spirituality, Science, and Surrender at the End of Life*, Brad Stuart, a doctor with long experience giving hospice care and treating terminal patients, expressed the challenge acerbically:

> Here's a brief factual summary of the current status of the human race from a strictly scientific viewpoint: humans are the product of a random process that has no cause. All our loves, hopes, and fears are the result of chance combinations of organic molecules. No individual act of heroic imagination, valiant action, or inspired striving

will last beyond the grave, except for the fading memories of survivors who won't last long themselves. All the
products of human genius are destined to vanish in the
frigid death of an expanding universe. How uplifting.

Speaking as a scientific materialist, I can aim answers
around questions of human purpose, to their left and right, but
I cannot strike them directly. I can say that it is better for us to
behave *as if* our lives are special and meaningful; that we are
constructed so that believing otherwise is not really possible
unless we're mentally unwell or on an acid trip. I can even say
there is something ineffably mysterious and beautiful about
human life which scientific, materialistic descriptions cannot
capture, although perhaps poetry and art can. Yet I cannot provide meaning and purpose which transcend oblivion.

Is that a problem? As I've said, not very much for me. I
feel exactly the same way as Richard Feynman, the American
physicist, who said, "I think it's much more interesting to live
not knowing than to have answers which might be wrong. . . .
I don't feel frightened by not knowing things, by being lost in
the mysterious universe without having any purpose—which
is the way it really is, as far as I can tell." But I am weird! Purely
secular thinking about death will never satisfy the large majority of people. Most rely on some version of faith to rescue them
from the bleak nihilism of mortality. Most believe we are here
for a reason; that our souls or essential beings transcend death;
that the universe was up to something special when it breathed
life into us. As William James argues in his seminal 1896 essay
"The Will to Believe," people have a perfect right to believe that
we exist for a reason, even if that reason is not scientifically
provable. We are, of course, not entitled to believe whatever we
please—that $2 + 2 = 5$, or that the world was created in six days,
or any other illogical or empirically false proposition; but in

those moral and spiritual areas which science cannot reach, we are just as entitled to accept the guidance of faith as to reject it. There is even a hypothesis that humans could not have made the evolutionary leap to intelligence had we not at the same time evolved religion to ease the otherwise unbearable knowledge of death. For all we know, *Homo sapiens* may have outcompeted other hominid species partly because we developed spiritualism to cope with the dread of mortality—whereas perhaps they did not.*

For a scientific materialist, anchoring morality poses a similar problem. To be more than expressions of personal taste, and to bind us even when no one is looking or when we can act with impunity, moral propositions—the Ten Commandments, the rules we learn in kindergarten, and all the rest— must have some external validity. Although we may never agree on *particular* moral precepts or on the specific source of their validity, it also cannot be adequate to define right and wrong in purely relativistic or aesthetic terms, such that there are no moral universals at all. The foundational problem posed by Plato in *The Republic*—why is there any unconditional reason to be good or just, or any reason to believe there is such a thing as goodness or justice?—requires an answer if we are to live with ourselves or (especially) with others in a non-sociopathic way.

Secular philosophers have worked very hard on Plato's problem. The logical positivists, such as A. J. Ayer, tried to define it out of existence by denying that moral claims have any meaning, so that the statement "murder is wrong" is just an emotional or aesthetic exclamation, an expression of distaste, no more rational than "Murder . . . *ugh!*" Unfortunately, positivism threw the baby out with the bathwater by denying the

---

*See Ajit Varki and Danny Brower, *Denial: Self-Deception, False Beliefs, and the Origin of the Human Mind* (Twelve, 2013).

possibility of moral reasoning, which leaves us worse off than ever. Another approach is observational. Certain moral traits seem wired into a healthy human psychology; certain moral tenets are common across human societies. Doesn't that make morality fundamental in some sense? Yes, but only in an empirical sense. To say a moral belief is ubiquitous is not to say it is right. Like slavery in the premodern world, it may be ubiquitous yet very wrong.

Titanic intellects like David Hume, Adam Smith, Charles Darwin, and Émile Durkheim—and their intellectual descendants, like Richard Dawkins and Sam Harris—have used scientific and naturalistic approaches to give us insights into the nature and evolution of human morals; but they anchor morality in ourselves and our societies, not in something transcendent. They may explain why I do not steal even if I can get away with it (sociability is necessary for survival, etc.), but they do not explain why I *must* not. They can say, correctly, that we will have happier lives if we think and act *as if* moral principles were universal and transcendent, but they cannot claim that any particular moral code *is* universal or transcendent.

Yet another approach is to yield to relativism: there is no absolute warrant for morality, and we just need to live with that—and anyway, religion, far from being reliably uplifting, often justifies the worst kind of immorality (slavery, again); so in the end, relativism is as functional as faith, perhaps more so. My own variant of relativism is that, even without access to absolute moral truths, moral *learning*—the objective advance of moral knowledge—is possible through reasoned criticism. We can say that the proposition "slavery is wrong" has been tested and justified by centuries of argument and evidence, in the same way that any other well-established proposition has been tested and justified—not with perfect certainty but with the confirmation of many lines of evidence and argument. From my secular, materialistic point of view, there is no absolute moral code inscribed in the stars, or at least there is none which is accessible to our imperfect minds; but that is true of all knowledge. Even without certainty, we still make moral progress in a systematic, non-arbitrary way, advancing our understanding of the moral world much as we advance our understanding of the material world—directionally *toward* truth, even if we never perfectly reach that goal. From the point of view of most people and most societies, however, relativism, even with my tweaks, is not adequate for strong, positive belief about good and evil. Escaping relativism and the moral chaos it can imply is the whole point.

So there is a lot of spaghetti which we on the secular side can throw against the wall by way of explaining why life has meaning and how moral claims are warranted. Having thrown it all, however, I am obliged to confess that purely secular thinking can get some distance toward putting mortality and morality on a solid footing, but it cannot get all the way there. It cannot answer the question, "If there is no transcendent moral order anchored in a purposive universe—something like God-given laws—why must we not be nihilistic and despairing sociopaths?"

Now, speaking as an atheist and a scientific materialist, I do not believe religions actually answer that question. Instead, they rely on a cheat, which they call God. They assume their conclusion by simply *asserting* the existence of a transcendent spiritual and moral order. They invent God and then claim he solves the problem. To me, that is not a solution; it is what philosophers call bootstrapping, a form of circularity. The Christians who believe the Bible is the last word on morality—and, not coincidentally, that *they* are the last word on interpreting the Bible—are every bit as relativistic as I am; it's just that I admit it and they don't.

That is neither here nor there. I am not important. What *is* important is that the religious framing of morality and mortality is plausible and acceptable to humans in a way nihilism and relativism are not and never will be. For most people, the idea that the universe is intended and ordered by God demonstrably provides transcendent meaning and moral grounding which scientific materialism demonstrably does not. I end up agreeing with Paul Nedelisky and James Davison Hunter in their book *Science and the Good: The Tragic Quest for the Foundations of Morality.* God may be (as I believe) a philosophical shortcut, but he gets you there—and I don't.

Murder and Miracles

But now we come to the other side of the equation, the other two M's. And here the religious side falls short.

In much the same way that secular philosophers have wrestled—nobly, insightfully, yet ultimately unsuccessfully— with the problem of morality, religious philosophers have wrestled with the problem of theodicy, often summarized as, "Why would a good God allow evil?"

My own atheistic view is that if something like God really existed, I would have to be against it. Not because God condemns us all to death; immortality sounds like a nightmare to me. But why, during life, torture us with diseases like the one which made my father—fully cognizant—choke on his own saliva? Why the cancer which took my friend Patricia's husband when their daughter was only a year old? Why the excruciating, chronic shingles which caused my friend Warren to lose hope and hang himself? Why typhoid, malaria, smallpox, and countless other diseases? Why the volcano which erased an entire city of 30,000 in Martinique in 1902? Why the tsunami which wiped out almost a quarter million souls in 2004? Does God really need to be so profligate a sadist? "As flies to wanton boys are we to the gods; they kill us for their sport."

The standard free-will argument, that God had to introduce evil into the world so that people could choose good, gets no traction against disease and natural disasters. Yet even more troubling is the problem of murder. When I was in college, a friend went out for a run and never came home. She was raped and murdered. I was shaken and angry then and remain shaken and angry today. Exercising free will was all well and good from the criminal's point of view, but why did God empower the murderer to exercise his free will by extinguishing hers? A caring God could easily have designed humans to feel far more averse to killing and harming others. He could have made us far more sensitive to the wounds we inflict and still have left us with meaningful choices. Instead, he created a world in which the Holocaust could happen; then he stood by when it did happen, and so did the millions who used their free will to choose complicity or turn a blind eye, mostly escaping accountability. One must ask oneself what kind of God would purchase the free will of Nazis at the price of six million Jewish lives. The claim that free will somehow justifies murder died at Auschwitz.

Confronted with that problem, God's defenders frequently retreat into mysticism. "We can't know why God does what he does and allows what he allows, but we should nonetheless assume he has a plan and it is good, because he is good." Obviously, this is no answer at all; it is merely a refusal to confront the question. To apply moral reasoning to our fellow humans while excusing God from all critical appraisal is to turn off our brains and license a capricious, sometimes monstrous divinity. It is, in the end, a dodge which excuses all kinds of violence and suffering as part of God's ineffable, unknowable plan. The universe cannot make moral sense if we accept the proposition that anything is okay if God does it.

A reason (one of many) I loved the late, great evangelical pastor and apologist Tim Keller is that he was candid about the problem of evil. He said theodicy is like a bucket. He could fill it with all the explanations and arguments he could think of, yet he could not make the bucket more than three-fourths full. Of course, atheists and materialists have no trouble accounting for the fact that bad things happen to good people, because we do not presume that the universe is fundamentally good. Instead, we dedicate ourselves to making it better. Similarly, we can cope with the fourth of the M's, miracles—an intractable and fundamental problem for religion.

In "Of Miracles" (Chapter 10 of his 1748 *Enquiry Concerning Human Understanding*), David Hume demolishes the possibility of miracles with a series of arguments which have never been successfully answered. Without saying so, Hume, an atheist, takes dead aim at the resurrection. By their very nature, he reasons, miracles violate the laws of nature; else they would not be miraculous. That means "there must . . . be a uniform experience against every miraculous event." In other words, to believe a miracle happened is to believe in what prior experience and known physical laws say is impossible. Moreover, Hume continues, there are always explanations which *are* consistent with experience and laws of nature; for example, that the supposedly miraculous event was misreported or misinterpreted, or faked, or never happened at all. Or perhaps there is some other explanation which is not yet known. If we hear of a miraculous event, therefore, it is *always* more rational to go with an explanation which experience shows to be possible than to bypass the possible and seize upon the impossible. Belief in the supernatural is exciting, Hume acknowledges: "The passion of surprise and wonder arising from miracles, being an agreeable emotion, gives a sensible tendency towards the belief of those events." But it can never be rationally justified, because any naturalistic explanation, however unlikely, is inherently more likely than any supernatural one.

Hume's argument, while sometimes framed as probabilistic, is really epistemic. The problem with magical thinking is not that "It's a miracle!" is merely an unlikely explanation for some event but that it is not an explanation at all. Rather, it is a negation of explanation. It waves aside all known regularities about the universe and admits any claim, however fanciful. If a shaman tells me she made it rain by placating angry spirits, I *must* disbelieve her: not because her account is improbable or even impossible, but because her account, if accepted, immediately makes nonsense of everything we know about meteorology, which in turn makes nonsense of everything we know about thermodynamics and chemistry and physics and even math and logic. If you assume even one miracle, then you can assume any number, and science becomes a game of Calvinball, a game without rules, where anyone can assert anything and chaos reigns. Worst of all, we are thrown into a world of incommensurable supernatural claims which no regular or rational process can adjudicate: a world of warring revelations and violent conflicts over competing supernatural dogmas— in other words, all of human history until the scientific revolution. The founding innovation of the scientific revolution was to demand explanations which are empirical, impersonal, replicable, and therefore socially adjudicable—thus placing magical thinking, including religious thinking, firmly out of bounds. In that way, belief in God, if God has any supernatural character, breaks the universe.

Obviously, many scientists are religious. They may believe that Jesus physically rose from the dead, but they do not look to exorcism to treat cancer. They somehow manage to accept supernaturalism in one part of life while rejecting it in another—an inconsistency I cannot accept, but so be it. My point here is not that you can't be a good scientist and also a good Christian; only that if you want a coherent, reliable, and socially adjudicable account of the material world, religious thinking cannot get you there. Pray and believe as your faith dictates, but when you are doing your scientific work, you must set aside your supernatural ideas and explanations and follow the rules of discovery and demonstration which I have elsewhere called the Constitution of Knowledge: rules which require us to treat only regular and replicable claims as objectively true. Even in principle, there is no theistic or spiritual path to a coherent, broadly shared, reliable, and progressively improving account of reality—no path, that is, to what we call *objective knowledge.*

The Cultural Trade Deficit

And so we wind up with two quite different modes of thinking, both inherently incomplete. A satisfactory account of the world requires both. A regime which subordinates one to the other, whether theocratic or Communistic, cannot be healthy or fully human.

Now, I want to draw some lines around my claims. I do not claim that only religious people can have strong, decent, and firmly anchored moral convictions. I do not claim that only secular people can have a firm grasp of objective reality. I do not claim that liberal democracy can't flourish amid secularization; Scandinavia and Japan (for example) show that it can, at least in high-trust, relatively homogeneous societies. What I do claim is that the four M's imply a certain division of labor— especially in America, which has traditionally relied on religion for so much of its cultural and spiritual infrastructure. The secular and religious worlds need not love each other or even quite understand each other, and at times they will be exasperated with each other. But they had better not actively undermine each other. Instead, they must foster conditions under which they can coexist.

Sometimes Christian America and secular America can rub along merely by leaving each other alone. But sometimes they come into conflict; and when they do, they have positive obligations to make room for each other. In other words, separation of church and state may fulfill the *legal* demands of our pluralist constitutional order; but from a moral and civic point of view, Christianity and secular liberalism are accountable not just to God and the Constitution respectively, but *to each other*. Their bargain requires that the Constitution be interpreted in a way which is consistent with the well-being of law-abiding faith communities, and that God's word be interpreted in a way which is consistent with the well-being of democratic pluralism. The bargain is implicit, but America depends upon it nonetheless.

The United States has been generally good at upholding this implicit bargain. America's demonstration that a country can be both devout and diverse, secular and spiritual, has been a historic achievement and a gift to the world. At least until recently, no other country or culture has accomplished it so well.

But the religious side has been less and less able to uphold its end of the bargain. That is what I mean by *thin* religion: too thin to provide meaning and morals to the culture and thus to reliably support democratic society. A result is what I think of as a cultural trade deficit.

Cultural trade deficit? Look at it this way. Secular liberalism certainly promotes important values: tolerance, lawfulness, civic responsibility, equality, and so forth. But they are primarily procedural values, which orient us to follow certain rules. The legitimacy of those rules must come largely from outside of secular liberalism itself (as, again, the Founders emphasized)—and, in practice, this has meant relying on Christianity to support the civic virtues. So we secular atheists rely on Christianity to maintain a positive cultural balance of trade: we need it to export more moral values and spiritual authority to the surrounding culture than it imports. If, instead, the church is in cultural deficit—if it becomes a net importer of values from the secular world—then it becomes morally derivative instead of morally formative. Rather than shaping secular values, it merely reflects them, and thus melts into the society around it. It becomes a consumer good, a lifestyle choice, or just another channel for politics—SoulCycle without the sweat, partisanship without the bunting and balloons.

You needn't take my word for it; Christians have been sounding alarms about the cultural trade deficit for years. "The church must stand against the way politics has become a religion, and religion has become politics," wrote Russell Moore in 2016, when he headed the Southern Baptist Convention's Ethics and Religious Liberty Commission. Others have warned of a dangerously diminished capacity to model Christian values for the culture. In 2017, Mark Labberton, then the president of Fuller Theological Seminary, said, "The church is in one of its deepest moments of crisis. Not because of some election result, but because of what has been exposed to be the poverty of the American church, in its capacity to be able to see and love and serve and engage in ways in which we simply failed to do."

"It's Destroying Hope"

And so where are we? David A. Hollinger puts it pithily in his 2022 book *Christianity's American Fate: How Religion Became*

More Conservative and Society More Secular. "The United States confronts a remarkable paradox," he writes: "*an increasingly secular society saddled with an increasingly religious politics.*"

At the turn of this century, I would have said that if Thin Christianity was bad for the church, that was no business of mine. I was smug about secularization ("apatheism"). As the country sank into chronic anomie and discontent, however, and as the public turned to dysfunctional and sometimes dangerous alternatives to religion, I began bending an ear to warnings that Christianity's crisis is democracy's, too. I came to realize that in American civic life, Christianity is a load-bearing wall. When it buckles, all the institutions around it come under stress, and some of them buckle, too. "Just as religion is damaged when the churches see themselves as political movements," wrote Joseph Bottum in the journal *First Things* in 2008, "so politics is damaged when political platforms act as though they were religions." Many others since then have repeated the warning. "If you're asking politics to solve your sense of moral purpose and character and meaning," said the *New York Times* columnist David Brooks in an online interview with Moore in 2022, "you're asking more of politics than it can bear."

On a winter day in 2022 I had the opportunity to ask Spencer Cox, the governor of Utah, about the challenges of governing. Cox is a conciliator by nature. As a newly appointed lieutenant governor in 2016, he took it upon himself to speak to an LGBT crowd holding vigil in Salt Lake City after the massacre at the Pulse nightclub in Orlando, Florida, took 49 lives. Instead of making vague expressions of sympathy, he owned up to his own past insensitivity to LGBT classmates and acquaintances: "I regret not treating them with the kindness, dignity, and respect—the love—that they deserved. For that, I sincerely and humbly apologize." Running for governor as a Republican in 2020, he cut a political ad with his Democratic opponent,

Chris Peterson, in which they attested to their shared values and promised to support the election's outcome. As chair of the National Governors Association in 2023, he launched a national initiative aimed at using governors' bully pulpits and convening power to encourage healthier disagreement.

"It's an unbelievably strong headwind," he told me, when I asked about governing in today's climate. Speaking of politics and media, he said: "The misalignment of incentives within those worlds, the algorithms and outrage cycles with social media and cable news, is incredibly degrading. It's destroying hope."

Then he turned to religion and the social connections it fosters. As people disaffiliate from faith, he said, "far too often we're replacing those connections with politics. Politics becomes our religion in many cases, and that harms our community and our souls. It makes governing inclusively much more difficult. My job would be so much easier if I woke up every morning and did whatever Fox News says that day."

That is the connection I missed two decades ago. Like it or not, the church's crisis is not only the church's business; it is Governor Cox's business, and indeed *my* business. Whether Christianity upholds its bargain with God is for God, not me, to say; but at present, as Americans abandon it in droves, it does not seem able to uphold its bargain with democracy.

We need to ask why. Is secular liberalism destroying religion, as liberalism's critics maintain? Does liberalism inevitably dissolve transcendent values in what Brink Lindsey calls an "acid bath of romantic hyper-individualism"?

Not all Christian voices think so. Recall what Russell Moore said in 2016: "The church must stand against the way politics has become a religion, and religion has become politics." And notice the subject of his sentence: *the church* must stand. Instead, it took a different direction.

2

Sharp Christianity
The Church of Fear
"Flight 93" evangelicalism betrays the church and the Constitution

Still bleary-eyed one morning in a hotel restaurant, I plop my breakfast plate down at a random table and strike up a conversation with the stranger sitting next to me. Since I am attending a conference on religion and civic life, I'm not surprised when he introduces himself as an evangelical pastor. I'll call him Mark. His church is Baptist, located in an oil town in west Texas. His congregants number about a hundred. Eighty percent are white, though the surrounding community is mostly Hispanic. "I love these people," he says of his parishioners. Yet when I ask if he has considered quitting the pastorate within the past year, he replies without hesitation. "*Absolutely.*"

Why? He uses a phrase which comes up several times in our conversation: *battlefield mindset.* His parishioners take an aggressive tone, one which reflects anger, fear: *Christianity is under attack and we have to do something about it.* They bring to church the divisive cultural issues they hear about on Fox News, such as critical race theory—even though, he tells me, many don't understand what that is.

And politics creeps in—not partisan campaigning as such, but a politicized, us-or-them worldview. "It's like talking to a wall with some people," Mark tells me, "because the Gospel is seen as political." The battlefield mindset is not new, but the 2016 presidential race and its aftermath "amped it up." Mark is worn down from hearing his white parishioners lament the loss of their country, so much so that he seeks out the company of his Hispanic friends outside church "because of what I *don't* have to talk about."

Will he continue in the pulpit? He takes it one day at a time. "I'm trusting God," he says. "There's a church within the church that really wants to follow Jesus." They're a minority, yet a reason to stay. "The gains are minimal, but you see them. But it's slow work."

Sixteen hundred miles from Pastor Mark, in the Washington, D.C., suburbs, Wayne (also not his real name), the pastor of an evangelical Presbyterian church, exhaustedly tells me he almost quit four times in recent years. "Theological belief has become a small factor in why people pick a church," he says. "People got more in love with their lifestyle than their faith." About ten years ago, he started to be bothered by a "snarkiness" and an "almost Nietzschean ethic" among his parishioners. "All of the stuff that has come to the fore was there but incipient"—and then the Trump phenomenon "turbocharged" it, roiling and dividing the congregation. "For our church, in the end, the center held," he says. But will comity survive the next political season? He shrugs. No way to know.

When I ask what the last few years have taught him, he replies, "I think we've learned that our congregation wasn't as spiritually mature as we thought it was." He frets about what he calls *spiritual rot.* I prod him: can't he, as pastor, do something about that? Isn't it his job to guide his flock spiritually?

"I can't make them want it," he sighs, with evident weariness. "That's the biggest challenge."

In rural North Carolina, a Baptist pastor tells me that fear and intolerance haunt his congregation, narrowing the range of acceptable belief. "In my opinion," he tells me, "the Baptist Faith and Message has become more like a noose. It's something that pastors have always faced, but I think it has become sharper in the last 20 years, and certainly within the last ten, and certainly after the election of Donald Trump. Trump spoke to some fears and incited fears. And when we're afraid, we don't always reach out in the most kind and loving ways." He tries to lead his congregation toward Jesus's capacious, forgiving message, but "I'm hired by a vote of the people and I'm fired by a vote, and there's no hierarchy to protect me from that. If congregants want a pastor to be removed, that's going to happen."

One can reproduce these conversations with pastors throughout the country. The words vary, but the tune is the same. Christian witness is in trouble in white evangelical America. And the biggest challenge is not from the secular world; it is sitting in the pews.

In Chapter 1, I spoke of the decline of white Christianity in America, both in numbers and in the church's loss of differentiation from the secular world outside—what I dubbed Christianity's cultural trade deficit. I explained why the "thinning" of Christianity is a hazard for democracy as well as a crisis for the church. I argued that secular society and religion are inherently and existentially interdependent; there is no secular substitute for the meaning and moral grounding which religious life provides. Yet Thin Christianity fails to provide the spiritual and communal anchors people need. I expressed alarm that Christianity seems less and less able, and less willing, to keep up its end of an implicit bargain with liberal democracy. And I argued that while church and state in America should not be allies as such, they must be to some significant extent aligned, or both will suffer.

In this chapter, I drill down into a central cause of today's misalignment, which I call Sharp Christianity: a divisive, fearful, partisan, and un-Christlike version of Christianity with dangerously illiberal implications. Although Sharp Christianity has many sources, including historical accident, demographic change, and challenges from the secular world, we should understand it, first and foremost, as a *choice* made by Christians—a catastrophic choice, because it corrodes not only democracy but also Christianity itself.

Before considering that thesis, though, we should take notice of its antithesis, which boasts a lot of followers and wins more every day.

Is Liberalism to Blame?

A loose constellation of ideas often called *post-liberalism* puts the shoe on the other foot, maintaining that Christianity and liberal democracy are indeed pulling apart, but Christians are not to blame. Rather, secular liberalism forced their hand; aggressive secularism relentlessly attacks and undermines Christian communities and other adherents of traditional values while also undermining democracy.

Liberalism is a broad church, with all kinds of variants and offshoots, and it offers many aspects for nuanced criticism. Unfortunately, post-liberalism is not generally interested in nuanced criticism. It paints with a broad brush, condemning the entire liberal tradition in sweeping terms. (In my crosser moods, I think of it as Blame Liberalism First.) Although post-liberalism has its own diversity of ideas and proponents, its anchoring premise is that liberalism is inherently self-under-mining because it cannot help but destroy the institutions and norms it depends on—among them, religion, faith, and the communal, traditional values which religion and faith sustain. The culprit is alleged to be an all-pervasive cult of individu-alism, a "me first" ideology which valorizes unbounded self-creation, personal liberty, cosmopolitanism, and consump-tion. One version of the case is summarized by Brink Lindsey of the Niskanen Center (who is a friendly critic of liberalism, not a post-liberal) in *The Permanent Problem,* his Substack blog:

> As America achieved mass affluence in the middle of the twentieth century, the romantic individualism of con-sumerism had become pervasive, and the percentage of people exposed to "highbrow" culture rose with the boom in college education. Conditions were ripe for Bohemia to become a mass phenomenon. Enter the 1960s, and the eruption of a youth rebellion—a "counterculture" that envisioned the coming of a bohemian millennium. . . . Anarcho-paradise never arrived, of course, and the ex-travagance of the antinomianism subsided. But the deep-seated hostility to authority and hierarchy of any kind, the tendency to regard established institutions as oppressive and illegitimate—that never went away.
>
> The acid bath of romantic hyper-individualism has degraded all the connections of contemporary society—connections to one's family, to all the major secular insti-tutions, to the land of one's birth, all the way to the shared sense of the sacred.

In his 2023 book *Freethinking: Protecting Freedom of Thought Amidst the New Battle for the Mind,* Simon McCarthy-Jones (also not a post-liberal) provides a concise summary of the post-liberal case:

> Post-liberal thinkers argue that liberalism is driven by the master value of autonomy. In such a society, freedom is the absence of any restraints. . . . Not only does autonomy have a price, but it actively undermines itself. Whereas in the eighteenth century people believed that obedience was the key to happiness, culture shifted and disobedience became the key to happiness. . . . Post-liberals point out that when we shatter norms, the wisdom of tradition, and the communities that historically regulated people's behavior, the state must step in to control the population. . . . Ironically, pursuing individual autonomy leads to centralized state power, which undermines individual autonomy.

An important aspect of this argument is its claim that liberalism is *inherently* self-destructive; it may pretend it is neutral, and may even believe it is neutral, but by its very nature it relentlessly promotes a radical individualism which bulldozes family, faith, and tradition. In his influential 2018 philippic *Why Liberalism Failed,* Patrick Deneen, a political theorist at the University of Notre Dame, declares: "Liberalism has failed—not because it fell short, but because it was true to itself. It has failed because it has succeeded. As liberalism has 'become more fully itself,' as its inner logic has become more evident and its self-contradictions manifest, it has generated pathologies that are at once deformations of its claims yet realizations of liberal ideology." Liberalism, he argues, "has drawn down on a preliberal inheritance and resources that once sustained liberalism but which it cannot replenish. The loosening of social bonds in nearly every aspect of life—familial, neighborly, communal, religious, even national—reflects the advancing logic of liberalism and is the source of its deepest instability."

Now, there is a softer, more nuanced critique which argues that liberalism has self-undermining *tendencies.* To which liberals can reply, "Yes, and you know this because we told you!" Ever since the seventeenth century, liberals have realized, and warned, that liberalism requires outside sources of support and stability. From the beginning, liberal theorists acknowledged that they did not attempt to prescribe an overarching concept of the good or of the purpose of life; rather, they left it up to individuals and civil society to define and supply those values, provided they did so non-coercively. Moral pluralism was a feature, not a bug, because the whole point of liberalism was to put an end to centuries of bloody coercion and war arising from religious and factional attempts to impose one group's moral vision on everyone else.

Liberalism thus challenges citizens and communities to develop "some shared account of the good life and the good community, and some way of forming good citizens who can exercise responsible freedom," as David P. Gushee puts it in his 2023 book *Defending Democracy from Its Christian Enemies.* That is no light burden. "It helped quite a bit that in the societies within which early democracies developed, the religious loyalties of the people were predominantly Christian," Gushee writes. "This religious, moral, and political background filled in much of the moral substance that was *intentionally* left out of liberal democratic constitutional documents. The kinds of people required to operate these new democratic systems—to govern well, to vote wisely, to debate civilly, to write good laws, to live with minimal state supervision—were produced by already-existing moral communities that inculcated moral virtues, values, and vision."

I italicized *intentionally* in the preceding quotation because the point is worth emphasizing: liberals understood they could not create and sustain virtue by themselves, and they warned against trying. As I noted in Chapter 1, the American Founders told everyone who would listen (and some who wouldn't) that the republic could not endure without a virtuous citizenry. They warned that the Constitution was necessary but not sufficient. Today, you will find similar warnings in the works of America's most prominent liberal thinkers, such as Francis Fukuyama, William Galston, and Peter Berkowitz. They have been outspoken about runaway individualism and woeful civic illiteracy, and they have proposed all sorts of measures, from civics education to political reforms, to make liberalism fairer and kinder. Sometimes I think that we at the Brookings Institution, the think tank where I work in Washington, D.C., do practically nothing else all day. To claim, then, that liberalism's shortcomings are a new discovery or unacknowledged by liberals is—well, cheeky, to say the least.

Going on four centuries after its origin, liberalism has defied every prediction of doom. It has somehow managed not to commit suicide. In some ways, it is more vigorous than ever. In the world as a whole, access to the Big Three liberal institutions— science, liberal democracy, and markets—is improving everyday life at an impressive speed, as a visit to the website *human progress.org* will quickly confirm. (Fact: "In 1950, the average [global] life expectancy at birth was only 48.5 years. In 2019, it was 72.8 years. That's an increase of 50 percent.") Still, point taken: we liberals should not be complacent about liberalism's problems or lazy about working to fix them—and too often, we are. Personal freedom and public-spiritedness will always be in tension; individualism and communitarianism will always require balancing; and sometimes the balance will be skewed— toward community, perhaps, in the 1950s, and toward individualism, perhaps, today.

Nonetheless, we can draw a fair distinction between constructive critiques of liberalism and the 192-proof versions which, traveling under the name *post-liberalism,* claim that liberalism is inherently, irreparably destructive to itself and to human flourishing. In this view, excessive individualism is not a challenging tendency, it is a fatal flaw. For post-liberalism, the seeds of liberalism's doom were present at the creation; society took a catastrophic wrong turn in the '60s—not the 1960s but the 1660s, when John Locke appeared on the scene. In a twist on Marxism, post-liberalism argues that today's democratic discontents are the working-out of liberalism's built-in contradictions and historical inevitabilities. The implication is that liberalism should be replaced with . . . well, with what, exactly? "For post-liberals, the common good, not autonomy, should be our master value," writes McCarthy-Jones. "This common good, they argue, can be objectively established."

The principle of Madisonian liberalism is that the common good cannot be divined objectively or authoritatively by any one person or faction. It must be constantly negotiated. In arguing for a society built on the one *true* idea of the common good, post-liberalism reverts to a pre-Madisonian tradition in which people look to the commands of God and the forms of Nature to anchor political authority. Here some problems arise.

Post-Liberal Pretentions

Detailing the infirmities of post-liberalism is not the purpose of this book; but we can briefly name some of them (there are others).

Straw-manning. Post-liberals set up liberalism as synonymous with libertinism, extreme libertarianism, and other forms of cultural hyper-individualism which mainstream liberalism neither entails nor accepts. According to the journalist

Sohrab Ahmari, for example, liberalism holds "that the goal of our common life together is to maximize the autonomy of the individual. If you wanted to boil down liberal theory to an axiom, it's no doubt that."* They mischaracterize John Locke and other liberal founders as enlisting government to smother tradition and to ignore the common good in the name of unconstrained individual liberty. "A main goal of Locke's philosophy," writes Deneen in *Why Liberalism Failed*, "is to expand the prospects for our liberty—defined as the capacity to satisfy our appetites—through the auspices of the state. . . . Thus one of the liberal state's main roles becomes the active liberation of individuals from any limiting conditions." Deneen has Locke backwards. Locke's great innovation was the idea of an implicit social contract, based on inherent natural rights, whereby free individuals agree to *constrain* the individual *and* the state, by restricting individuals' freedom to dominate each other and restricting the state's freedom to dominate individuals. "Locke's fundamental moral and political premise—that human beings are by nature free and equal—imposes significant limits on individual conduct and government," writes Berkowitz in his review of *Why Liberalism Failed*.† If you want to see rampant suppression of communities and traditions, just look to the countless illiberal regimes which have quashed and persecuted anything not within the state-approved community and tradition. And Ahmari's claim that liberalism's central "axiom" is to maximize individual autonomy at the expense of everything else is a caricature, unrecognizable to liberal theorists except as a red herring. The American Founders understood very well

---

* Interview with Yascha Mounk, August 12, 2023, available at www.per suasion.community/p/ahmari.

† Peter Berkowitz, "Anti-Liberal Zealotry Part III: Locke and the Liberal Tradition," *RealClearPolicy.com,* September 21, 2018.

the difference between license and ordered liberty, and between unfettered autonomy and delineated rights; they wrote
the Constitution precisely for that reason. "Let it be remem-
bered," John Jay wrote in famous instructions to a grand jury,
"that civil liberty consists not in a right to every man to do just
what he pleases, but it consists in an equal right to all the citizens to have, enjoy, and to do, in peace, security, and without
molestation, whatever the equal and constitutional laws of the
country admit to be consistent with the public good." Liberalism is premised on supremacy of law and restraint of ego, not
supremacy of self and elevation of ego.

Catastrophism. Like Marxism, post-liberalism underval-
ues, ignores, or takes for granted the unparalleled economic,
scientific, social, and moral advances of liberalism: important
things like constitutional democracy, mass prosperity, the scientific revolution, outlawing slavery, empowering women, and—
not least from my point of view—tolerating atheistic homosexual Jews instead of burning us alive. Post-liberalism's descriptions
of liberal societies resemble modern America about as much
as Donald Trump's descriptions of urban hellscapes resemble
actual U.S. cities. Patrick Deneen is willing to grant (in a hand-
ful of asides) that liberalism achieved some real triumphs in
the past—but, he writes, "nearly every one of the promises that
were made by the architects and creators of liberalism has been
shattered." Really? What about unprecedented peace, prosperity, knowledge, freedom, and respect for human rights? Personally, I would rather live in any liberal, market-based democracy
than in one of the theocratic, socialist, monarchist, or authoritarian alternatives, and I suspect most of America's post-liberal professoriate would too.

Authoritarianism. Well, maybe some post-liberals would
prefer to live in Hungary. Not surprisingly, those who reject
liberalism as too individualistic, permissive, and irreligious ro-

manticize the illiberal alternatives—and they show up in Budapest celebrating the likes of Hungarian prime minister Viktor Orbán, a self-proclaimed advocate of "illiberal democracy" and leader of a global authoritarian-populist movement to undermine democracy. Post-liberals charge that liberalism's commitment to neutrality is a sham, covering up (according to Deneen) a "more insidious" agenda which "surreptitiously remakes the world in its image." But liberalism claims to be neutral only with respect to state procedures such as laws and elections. There is nothing "neutral" about its *values,* such as its core precept that all people are born free and equal. If that precept is the "image" in which liberalism "surreptitiously remakes the world," I'll gladly take it over Orbán.

Make-believe. In keeping with their authoritarian bent, post-liberals seem to imagine a world in which they can wield government authority without interference from other factions—say, progressives, moderates, and libertarians. Worse, they seem to imagine a world in which today's deep political and cultural divisions somehow subside, allowing them to bypass democracy's give-and-take and impose their conservative preferences (which they call the "common good," ignoring competing accounts of the common good). We have a word for such post-political daydreaming: *wishcasting.* In a modern country of 350 million very different people, political and moral disagreement is intrinsic, and some version of liberalism—in our case, James Madison's—is the only system which has proved capable of managing it.

Incoherence. Post-liberalism has no theory of government—or, rather, it has too many theories. Is the state too big and powerful, or too small and weak? That depends. When addressing individual rights, the state is overweening, leveling, and dependency-inducing. When addressing the "common good," the state needs to be more bold and assertive. Which is it? Post-liberalism seems to slide back and forth as convenience dictates. Also, which aspects of liberal individualism would post-liberals retain, and which would they throw away? Women's equality? Gay rights? Why or why not? Without a coherent theory, we have only their personal preferences.

Vagueness. A critique of modern liberalism needs to tell us, concretely and specifically, what regime is better. What country or state, past or present, is their model? Illiberal democracy, like Orbán's Hungary? Religious nationalism, as in Modi's India? Some sort of Catholic social democracy like—well, like where? Post-liberalism doesn't tell us. "What is most striking about their commitment to what they call classical and Christian values, constantly reiterated in their books," the political theorist Michael Walzer observed in a 2023 interview with Yascha Mounk, "is that they never give us a concrete description of the society in which they think those values prevail. And it would be in the classical cases a society of slavery and war; it would be a society of persecution of heretics, the Inquisition, the pogroms of the Crusades against Jews and then Muslims; deep poverty [and] hierarchy."

Grandstanding. Post-liberals are not shy about declaring liberalism a failure and calling for radical change. (Patrick Deneen has claimed to stand for "regime change," something "far more revolutionary" than the violent overthrow of the U.S. government.* Really?) But when they get down to brass tacks, they proffer a grab-bag of small-bore suggestions which (thank goodness) hardly live up to their revolutionary billing: symbolic government moralism like Sunday closing laws, "pro-worker" policies like reshoring and stricter antitrust rules, communitarian standbys like national service, boilerplate political

---

* Ian Ward, "'I Don't Want to Violently Overthrow the Government. I Want Something Far More Revolutionary,'" *Politico Magazine,* June 8, 2023.

reforms like expanding the House of Representatives, and a call for conservatives to repopulate elite cultural institutions, whatever that means. One can argue about the worth of such ideas, but none of them is incompatible with liberal constitutionalism or requires "regime change."

In the end, post-liberalism snags itself on a dilemma: its post-liberal ideas are not practical and its practical ideas are not post-liberal. If it wishes to be more than vaporware and become a governing philosophy, it must drop its radical pretentions and content itself with reforms which comport with America's founding traditions; if it wishes to advertise itself as a radical alternative to the whole liberal order, it marginalizes itself with authoritarian daydreaming.

So What Is Christianity's Problem?

Despite post-liberalism's infirmities, liberals can learn from it if we divide its criticisms by ten. I don't mean that comment snidely. Post-liberalism, like critiques going back to Nietzsche (and Plato), does have something to teach us about the challenges facing secular democracies and economies—and, yes, about the challenges which consumerism and individualism and neoliberalism and all the other "isms" pose for religious institutions and traditional values. We need to grant that today's fast-changing, media-addicted, materialistic, liberationist America is not an easy environment for conservative faiths like evangelical Christianity.

Yet it is not possible to blame the troubles of American Christianity solely or even mainly on rampant, aggressive secularism. Consumerism and individualism did not arrive recently; religious figures have been complaining about mammon and cupidity in American life for generations. The mid-twentieth century provided a stable, culturally conservative consensus in which institutional religion could flourish, but that period was exceptional. Until recently, the United States rightly prided itself on how its pluralism fostered the world's most vibrant marketplace of religions. Americans loved to brag that we owe our religious dynamism not to stagnant state churches, as in Europe, but to the very freedoms which post-liberals now bemoan. Whatever changed for Christianity seems to be of recent vintage, postdating the 1960s by decades and accelerating sharply in the past decade or so.

Do capitalism and consumerism and individualism pose challenges for Christianity? Sure; but let's not forget that they create opportunities too, by increasing the demand for spiritual anchors in a turbulent world. We see this in the soaring demand for pseudo-religions in American life, as well as in the success of evangelicalism in the developing world. As Micklethwait and Wooldridge point out in *God Is Back,* "Faith provides certainty in a world where secular certainties are constantly being undermined. . . . People everywhere, but particularly in the developing world, are reacting to the hurricane of capitalism by taking cover under the canopy of religion." Christianity is thriving and growing in much of the Global South—apparently by offering what people want. Why not in America?

We cannot answer that question by focusing only on the challenges of secularism. Instead, we need to listen to Benjamin Franklin: "When religion is good, I conceive it will support itself; and when it does not support itself, and God does not take care to support [it], so that its professors are obliged to call for help of the civil power, 'tis a sign, I apprehend, of its being a bad one."

In other words, we need to consider the role Christianity has played in its own demise.

The Church of Social Justice

If we wanted to summarize the direction of change in American Christianity over the past century or so, we might do well to use the term *secularization.*

Secularization does not necessarily imply that theology melts away, believers stop believing, churches empty out, and clergy compromise their principles. Up to a point, it can mean cross-pollination as religions interact with their social environments and become less countercultural, with both sides often benefiting from the exchange. In its ill-mannered way, the musical *The Book of Mormon* makes a shrewd observation: religion works best when it adapts to meet the needs of real people. I can speak for many gay and Jewish Americans, and also many women and for that matter Christians, in maintaining that secular influence has helped Christianity become more tolerant, more reality-based, and ultimately more Christlike. Whether secularization is a good or bad thing depends on what is being secularized, by whom, and how.

So, again, secularization is not a dirty word—up to a point. Yet students of religion have persuasively argued that the secularization of both mainline American Protestantism and white evangelical Protestantism went beyond that point, albeit in very different ways.

The story generally told about the mainline, or ecumenical, church is that the first half of the twentieth century brought new challenges. As David A. Hollinger argues in *Christianity's American Fate,* missionary work abroad opened the church's eyes to global issues, while urbanization, immigration, and education shattered its complacency at home. Protestantism found itself confronting "a demographically diverse, sexually and racially egalitarian, globally engaged, and scientifically literate society welcoming to Jews and to other non-Christians." The civil rights movement and the rise of liberation theology brought further calls for the church to engage with issues like poverty and racism.

While conservative evangelicalism tried to fend off such influences, mainline churches, to their credit, attempted to meet them. Seminaries, divinity schools, and pulpits reflected the progressive values of the politically liberal world. Ecumenical churches' membership reached an all-time high at mid-century, but their commitments were increasingly social, not theological. "One way to join the establishment," Hollinger writes, "was to go to the right church, or to say that you did." Meanwhile, "the ecumenical intelligentsia made little effort to plant their own flag in the Bible. This decision to hold back is one of the most remarkable choices made in the entire history of the campaign for a more cosmopolitan Protestantism."

In a well-intentioned gamble, the mainline church cast its lot with center-left progressivism and let itself drift, or at least seem to drift, from scriptural moorings. In 1996, the religious historian Randall Balmer damned Protestant ecumenicism as "so careful not to offend that its blandness has become an affront. In the eyes of many Americans mainline Protestants have become so intent on blurring theological and denominational distinctiveness that they stand for nothing at all, aside from some vague (albeit noble) pieties like peace, justice, and inclusiveness."*

However noble the mainline church's intentions, as it became more a cultural institution than a spiritual one, its distinctiveness faded. At the same time, it lost its hold on social life; people stopped placing one another on the social ladder by asking which church they belonged to, and started asking

* Randall Balmer, *Grant Us Courage: Travels Along the Mainline of American Protestantism* (Oxford University Press, 1996), 148.

where they worked and went to college. The cultural revolts of
the 1960s and 1970s, followed by mass religious disaffiliation,
only compounded the church's irrelevance, leading to the melt-
down it experienced in the late twentieth and early twenty-first
centuries.

Although I am neither a Christian nor a progressive, I
would love to see a revival of mainline Christianity. Its values
and aspirations strike me as noble. Also, as Joseph Bottum and
others have argued, the collapse of the ecumenical churches
has displaced religious zeal into politics, which is not designed
to provide purpose in life and breaks when it tries. I am not
saying ecumenical Christianity can make a comeback, or will;
but it is far from dead, and hope springs eternal.

Meanwhile, the evangelical side of the church also became secularized, taking a more radical and perilous path.

The Partisan Church

A Republican presidential candidate—one whose apparent extremism alarms not just liberal Democrats but also many establishment Republicans—sits to be interviewed by a prominent
evangelical and rhetorically asks: "Do you ever get the feeling
sometimes that if we don't do it now, if we let this be another
Sodom and Gomorrah, that maybe we might be the generation
that sees Armageddon?" Agreeing, the evangelist replies, "This
is the most important election ever to face the United States. I
really believe that. . . . I don't think anyone knows what has
happened in our leadership in the crushing of religion in this
country."

Donald Trump and Franklin Graham in 2020? No, Ronald Reagan and Jim Bakker in 1979.

The effective merger of the American evangelical movement with the Republican Party is not new. One can trace its

roots back to the first half of the twentieth century, when conservative evangelicals split from moderate and progressive ecumenicals; then, in the 1960s, to the civil rights movement, which many Southern evangelicals rejected. (Asked to comment on Martin Luther King's 1968 "I have a dream" speech, the evangelist Billy Graham said, "Little white children of Alabama will walk hand in hand with little black children only when Christ comes again." By which he didn't mean soon.) In the 1970s, realizing they could co-opt the racialized, resentful energy George Wallace had tapped, Republican strategists unrolled the welcome mat to white Southern conservatives, including evangelicals. I am old enough to remember when Jimmy Carter, a born-again Christian and a moderate Democrat, could win the presidency with evangelical support. But that was in 1976. By 1980, the Republicans' Southern strategy was firmly established, and realignment was a juggernaut.

In those days, Republican strategists assumed they could manage their new evangelical converts without fundamentally reshaping the party. They supposed that Christian conservative voters could be bought off with symbolic, usually half-hearted gestures like platform planks calling for prayer in public schools. Similarly, evangelical leaders believed their partisan alignment could be managed without fundamentally reshaping the church. Evangelicals would influence the party more than it would influence them. Both assumptions proved wrong.

By the turn of this century, white evangelicals constituted the biggest and most loyal element of the Republican political base. In 2004, according to exit polls, 79 percent of them voted for George W. Bush; in 2012, the same share cast their ballots for Mitt Romney (a member of the Church of Jesus Christ of Latter-day Saints). Even John McCain, a less conventionally conservative figure, received almost three-fourths of the white evangelical vote in 2008.

"Despite their declining share of the electorate since the beginning of the twenty-first century," write the Brookings Institution's E. J. Dionne and William Galston, "white evangelicals continue to represent a formidable voting bloc. They constitute about 30 percent of Republican identifiers as well as 14 percent of the electorate."* It is no exaggeration to say that Republicans cannot win nationally without white evangelicals' support. For most intents and purposes, the white evangelical movement has become a one-party town. According to the religious demographer Ryan Burge, "White evangelicalism has never been more politically unified than it is right now. In the 1970s, only 40 percent of white weekly churchgoing evangelicals identified as Republicans; in the most recent data, that number has risen to an all-time high of 70 percent."†

The bond was more than an electoral alliance; political and religious messaging merged, too. "From 1976 onward," writes Thomas S. Kidd in his 2019 book *Who Is an Evangelical? The History of a Movement in Crisis,* "'evangelical' would increasingly connote the white religious Republican base." An apt and quite un-endearing symbol of the merger of church and party was a Christmas image posted in 2021 by a Republican congressman showing his whole family posing in front of a Christmas tree with military-style rifles.‡ (Is that what Jesus would do?)

If the political union of white evangelical Christianity with

---

* E. J. Dionne, Jr., and William A. Galston, "How Younger Voters Will Impact Elections: What Is Happening to the White Evangelical Vote?" The Brookings Institution, June 27, 2023.

† Ryan Burge, "Why 'Evangelical' Is Becoming Another Word for 'Republican,'" *New York Times,* October 26, 2021.

‡ Joey Garrison, "Andy Ogles, GOP Congressman Representing Nashville Shooting Site, Criticized for Posing with Guns in Family Christmas Photo," *USA Today,* March 27, 2023.

Republican partisanship began as a marriage of convenience, it soon evolved into codependency. Perhaps inevitably, partisanship backflowed into the church, causing a spiral in which white conservative Republicans self-selected into evangelical religious identities and those identities in turn reinforced the church's partisanship. In her 2018 book *From Politics to the Pews: How Partisanship and the Political Environment Shape Religious Identity,* Michele F. Margolis argues against the standard idea that religious belief drives partisan political preferences. Rather, there is a reciprocal relationship in which partisanship also drives religious identification. The spiral, she writes, can become self-propelled: "If partisans select into or out of religious communities, in part, based on their political outlooks, they will find themselves in more politically homogeneous social networks where they encounter less diverse political information. Rather than churches being places where people with different political viewpoints come together, religious communities may become more like echo chambers populated by like-minded partisans." Sharp Christianity intensifies partisanship, which further sharpens Christianity. And what if partisan politics becomes the main reason people choose to identify as evangelicals? Could party loyalty elbow Jesus aside? Could evangelical Christianity become, for many who affiliate with it, primarily a political rather than religious identity?

That appears to have happened. "Instead of theological affinity for Jesus Christ, millions of Americans are being drawn to the evangelical label because of its association with the GOP," writes Burge. "Now the data indicate that more and more Americans are conflating evangelicalism with Republicanism— and melding two forces to create a movement that is not entirely about politics or religion but power." Perhaps especially telling is that, according to Burge, the share of self-identified evangelicals who attend church "seldom or never" rose from about 10 percent in 2008 to more than a fourth in 2020. In 2021, the Pew Research Center found that "there has been no large-scale departure from evangelicalism among white Americans"— but this was because an inflow of Trump supporters began identifying as evangelical, "perhaps reflecting the strong association between Trump's political movement and the evangelical religious label."*

Looking at such data, Burge suggested in a 2021 *New York Times* article that "'evangelical' is not a religious term anymore." Prominent evangelicals have made the same point. "The kind of cultural Christianity we now see often keeps everything about the Religious Right except the religion," wrote Russell Moore in *Christianity Today* (where he became editor after stepping down as head of the Southern Baptist Convention's Ethics and Religious Liberty Commission).† Peter Wehner, of the Trinity Forum, observed in a 2022 interview with *American Purpose* that "a spiritual outlook has been replaced by a core identity that's political." Whereas churches used to argue about doctrinal matters, he added, "it's now things like critical race theory or Disney or where you stand on Trump or masks or vaccines. That's something new and very worrisome."‡ Curtis Chang, a scholar and former pastor, told me bluntly: "At this point, 'evangelical' is a political uniform; it's code for politically conservative."

---

* Gregory A. Smith, "More White Americans Adopted Than Shed Evangelical Label During Trump Presidency, Especially His Supporters," Pew Research Center, September 15, 2021.

† Russell Moore, "When the South Loosens Its Bible Belt," *Christianity Today*, August 11, 2022.

‡ Available at www.youtube.com/watch?v=N1Orn_Zu4_8.

Unforced Error

One might be inclined to blame the secular culture for white evangelicalism's embrace of political partisanship. Evangelicals' values (runs this argument) have been under siege by the secular world and the political left; were conservatives supposed to sit there and suck their thumbs? Perhaps (this argument continues) some might expect conservative Christians to meekly accept the industrial-scale murder of unborn children, the aggressive promotion of LGBT ideology, the left's intolerance of traditional social mores, and the relentless advance of wokeness in universities, corporations, and the media; but enough is enough. It is both natural and biblical for Christians to stand up for their values.

One problem with this view is that the idea of a relentless legal attack on Christianity is fanciful. Never before in American history have the law and the Supreme Court been as protective of religious liberty as they are right now. As the historian and evangelical Paul Matzko said (in a podcast interview with *The UnPopulist* in 2022), "Conservative American Christians are not just the least persecuted religious community in the world today, they're arguably the least actually persecuted religious community in all of human history." As I drafted this paragraph, the Supreme Court had just delivered the latest in a string of victories for freedom of religion and conscience, ruling that commercial creative enterprises can turn away business which requires them to express ideas they object to. A Christian-owned web designer has a constitutional right to refuse service for a same-sex wedding. The court has affirmed the ministerial exemption in religious-based hiring; it has blessed the flow of public tax dollars to private religious schools; it has exempted giant corporations in secular industries from government regulations on religious grounds; on and on. "In fact," wrote the lawyer and commentator (and evangelical) David French, in a 2022 article for *The Dispatch*, "religious freedom is enjoying a decade-long winning streak at the Supreme Court, with most of the key cases decided through right-left super-majorities."

No doubt, activists on the secular left would like to withdraw federal tax deductions and contracts from faith-based charities which discriminate against LGBT people; but in 2022, in the Respect for Marriage Act, Congress repudiated such efforts—with the unanimous support of Democrats. Respect for freedom of conscience is at the core of liberalism; and accommodation for freedom of religion is specifically enshrined in the Constitution, as well as in the 1993 Religious Freedom Restoration Act. Polling by the Pew Research Center in 2023 found that only 27 percent of Americans took an unfavorable view of evangelicals, and disapproval of mainline Protestants and Catholics was even lower. America is anything but a combat zone for Christianity. The "war on Christmas" is entirely made up.

"Well," some Christians might reply, in defense of the proposition that their faith is embattled, "maybe the law is protective of religious freedom. Maybe the general public isn't out to get us. But you can't deny that cultural elites treat conservative white Christians as deplorables. Christians are constantly demeaned and condemned. It's natural and justifiable for us to push back."

That is true to an extent. You won't find a lot of conservative evangelicals in Harvard faculty meetings or the *New York Times* newsroom (though you will find some). But moral conviction is a two-way street, and conservative evangelicals are not the only ones with values to defend. To the extent that the progressive cultural establishment abhors conservative evangelicals, it does so mainly because of their conservatism, not their Christianity. From a secular, progressive point of view, white conservative evangelicals' history of opposing fundamental human rights for blacks, women, and sexual minorities is shameful, as is their opposition to abortion rights today. Right or wrong, the progressives' claims have substantive moral weight and should not be personalized as expressions of anti-Christian bigotry.

But let us set that caveat aside. Let's grant that America's secular culture has been adversarial to conservative Christian values. Let's grant, too, that the secular left has been aggressive and successful in moving the Overton window in its direction, especially on cultural issues. (Homosexual people like me are a huge beneficiary, and we don't apologize.) Let's grant that the country is drifting toward godlessness, that Christians are headed toward minority status, that the country is diversifying away from white Protestant preeminence. How should white evangelicals respond? With political activism, yes. Perhaps even some degree of partisanship, up to a point.

We can debate where that point is; but there came a moment when that point was passed and then left far behind. Absolutely nothing about secular liberalism required white evangelicals to embrace the likes of Donald Trump.

A Choice and a Change

As familiar as the facts became during the decade when Trump dominated the U.S. political landscape, we might still remind ourselves how he inverted what were once understood as core Christian values. He entered the national policy conversation in 1989 by taking out full-page ads in four New York City newspapers demanding that the state adopt the death penalty for five black teenagers, saying, "I want to hate these murderers and I always will," and he did not change his stance when they were later proven innocent. He made his debut in national politics by slurring a black presidential candidate as not American. As president, he demanded that two black congresswomen, both born in the United States, "go back" to "the places from which they came." He bragged that, as a celebrity, he could "grab [women] by the pussy," and a jury subsequently found he had done exactly that. He diverted funds from his putative charity for personal use and was forced by a court to acknowledge the scam. In his business, he routinely stiffed his contractors. His company was found guilty of criminal and civil tax fraud. He lied his way to the presidency: 70 percent of his fact-checked statements in the 2016 campaign were found by PolitiFact to be mostly or entirely false. He lied his way *through* the presidency: his first two acts as president were to lie about the size of his inaugural crowd and whether it rained during his inauguration; thereafter, according to the *Washington Post*'s fact checkers, he perpetrated an average of 20 falsehoods a day. His post-election "Stop the Steal" campaign constituted the most audacious and successful disinformation attack ever mounted against our country by any actor, foreign or domestic. He tried to end our democracy by attempting to overturn an election, refused to acknowledge the possibility of his fair defeat, told far-right militia groups to "stand back and stand by" for insurrection, incited mob violence at the Capitol (and told the mob he "loved" them), placed his own vice president in mortal danger, encouraged thugs to defame and menace election officials, and explicitly called for the "termination of all rules, regulations, and articles, even those found in the Constitution"—which, if his corrupt scheme to overturn the 2020 election had succeeded, he might have achieved.

Knowing all that, one must also recall that his signature characteristic, his political specialty, and his one true genius was his sociopathic cruelty. He called women things like "horseface," said they were too ugly to rape, and ridiculed them for menstruating; he mocked the heroic and the handicapped; he humiliated his rivals with epithets and his loyalists with indignities. Basic decency was foreign to him, and fellow humans mere outlets for his monstrously fragile ego.

Yet Trump won more than 80 percent of the evangelical vote in 2016, more than George W. Bush (an avowed born-again), John McCain, or Mitt Romney. Although white evangelicals were initially wary of him, the die was cast as early as January 2016, when he traveled to an evangelical college in Iowa to make a promise. "Christianity will have power," he said. "If I'm there, you're going to have plenty of power, you don't need anybody else. You're going to have somebody representing you very, very well. Remember that."

They did remember—not, apparently, minding that in the very same speech he mocked and exposed them by bragging that they would support him even if he shot someone on Fifth Avenue. If ever there was a Mephistophelian moment in American politics, that was it.

Mephistopheles was good at rationalizing, and evangelicals offered many rationalizations for the deal they made with Trump. *He was better than Hillary Clinton.* Perhaps so, in November 2016; but that did not explain evangelicals' redoubled support for him long after Hillary Clinton had left the scene. *He made good Supreme Court appointments.* Other Republicans would have chosen from the same list, which was assembled by the Federalist Society and handed to him. *He was running for president, not preacher.* Trump was not a hypocrite who sinned in private; his cruelty and shamelessness defined not only his personality but his policies and rhetoric. He endorsed torture, stealing oil, and murdering alleged terrorists' relatives; tore howling babies from the arms of migrant parents (as of this writing, about 1,000 families had not been reunited); mused about shooting migrants in the legs; used military aid for political blackmail; pardoned duly convicted war criminals; encouraged violence against journalists and protesters. One would have thought that, for Christians, his prideful cruelty might have disqualified him as both preacher *and* president.

Before Trump's emergence, the evangelical world had insisted that character matters—even though presidents aren't preachers. In a 2016 poll headlined "Backing Trump, White Evangelicals Flip-Flop on Importance of Candidate Character," the Public Religion Research Institute (in collaboration with Religion News Service and the Brookings Institution) noted that in 2011, when Barack Obama was president, only 30 percent of white evangelicals said that "an elected official who commits an immoral act in their personal life can still behave ethically and fulfill their duties in their public and professional life." Five years later, when Donald Trump led the Republican presidential ticket, *72 percent* of white evangelicals gave personal immorality a pass. Among American religious groups, white evangelicals had switched from being the least accepting of personal immorality among public officials to being the *most* accepting. Something had changed, and it probably was not the Gospel.

Sophisticated Christians rationalized support for Trump by calling him a kind of necessary evil, or, in the words of Os Guinness, "God's wrecking ball stopping America in its tracks [from] the direction it's going and giving the country a chance to rethink." In this view, a vote for Trump was less a positive endorsement than an effort to prevent a true catastrophe in the form of Hillary Clinton. Although not lacking in sense, this argument had a couple of deficiencies. One was that, back in the not-so-ancient Bill Clinton era, evangelicals had maintained that bad character was disqualifying in its own right, not just conditionally, and they had derided what was sometimes called "compartmentalization" of the president's moral defects. A deeper problem was that conservative Christians could have chosen to accept Trump reluctantly while vigorously calling out his depravity and seeking and supporting better alternatives.

The poll results suggested, however, that one could set aside the rationalizations. Few white evangelicals even bothered with them. Most did not support Trump reluctantly. They were not temporizing until a less crude, corrupt, and cruel alternative emerged (because, of course, there were many such alternatives, starting with his vice president). They did not merely support Trump, they *adored* him. He was a warrior, a champion who said aloud what others merely thought, who made progressives tremble with rage. Sure, maybe he was "rough around the edges," but here at last was a leader who *fights*. When he deployed tear gas to disperse lawful protesters for a photo op in which he stood in front of a church (which he did not enter) and held up a Bible (which he did not pretend to have opened), I saw an obvious charlatan, but his Christian supporters seemed thrilled. They seemed to regard even his insincerity as a form of tribute.

"Evangelicals were looking for a protector, an aggressive, heroic, manly man, someone who wasn't restrained by political correctness or feminine virtues, someone who would break the rules for the right cause," writes Kristin Kobes Du Mez, in her 2020 book *Jesus and John Wayne*. "In fact, the more unconventional, bombastic, and offensive he became, the more evangelicals seemed to rally to his side." Today, when white evangelicals have seen so many depravities from Trump and MAGA and have forgone so many opportunities to rethink their loyalty, it is not possible to avoid the truth of her conclusion: "In 2016, many observers were stunned at evangelicals' apparent betrayal of their own values. In reality, evangelicals did not cast their vote despite their beliefs, but because of them."

Was conservative white Christians' embrace of Trump a natural culmination of decades-long trends? Or was it a break with the past? The answer has to be: some of both. Many authorities emphasize continuity. Du Mez notes that bully-worship did not appear in the church out of nowhere:

> Evangelical support for Trump was no aberration, nor was it merely a pragmatic choice. It was, rather, the culmination of evangelicals' embrace of militant masculinity, an ideology that enshrines patriarchal authority and condones the callous display of power, at home and abroad. By the time Trump arrived proclaiming himself their savior, conservative white evangelicals had already traded a faith that privileges humility and elevates "the least of these" for one that derides gentleness as the province of wusses.

Similarly, David Hollinger concludes: "Contrary to the view that evangelicalism is a benign presence in American life, hijacked by outsiders, I argue that evangelicalism's history prepared it to be just what it showed itself to be in the era of Donald Trump."

No doubt, the predicates of the First Church of MAGA had been developing for a long time. By the time Trump came along, the church's partisan cast and paranoid disposition had made the evangelical world receptive. True—but *dis*continuity deserves the greater emphasis. Trump's violations of Christian ethical norms, his cruelty and crudity and bullying and lying, went far beyond any precedent in American politics. Even George Wallace was a gentle country deacon by comparison. Trump was a next-level phenomenon, and white evangelicals' decision to make him their champion was not implied by their history up to that point. Having been cool to him initially, they could very well have rejected him as too much of a bad thing. They might have questioned what their effective merger with the Republican Party was doing to their church and their souls. Instead they doubled down—again and again. One was left to conclude that Trump had been right in Iowa: there seemed to be no misbehavior which his white evangelical base could not rationalize or overlook. And this was something no one could have foreseen. Whatever the predicates, embracing Trump and MAGA was fundamentally a choice and a change.

Witnessing that choice, shocked by it, I lost my hard-won faith. Not in God, but in Christians. In my youth, I had been an atheist of the militant, angry variety. I had seen little but hypocrisy and cruelty in Christianity. But then I got to know Christians who walked the walk. I came to appreciate that there was a radically self-effacing and kind side to Christian doctrine, and that even the doctrines I disagreed with (such as the condemnation of homosexuality) could, in principle, be defended in good faith on scriptural grounds. During the gay marriage debate, I assured my LGBT friends that Christians on the other side weren't bigots and haters, at least not usually; that even when wrong, they were sincerely trying to follow God's word as they understood it. I said, "They may be wrong, but they aren't mean."

The Trump phenomenon made me doubt all that. My breaking point came in April 2020, when Albert Mohler, a leading Southern Baptist authority whose integrity I had taken seriously, endorsed Trump for reelection despite having rejected him in 2016 as "beneath the baseline level of human decency."* At that point, I had to throw in the towel. I had to accept that my younger self and my LGBT friends had been right—if not

* In 2023, Mohler said he would not support Trump in the Republican primaries.

entirely, than in dismayingly great measure. The majority of white evangelicals followed a leader who was not even a little like Jesus. Cruelty and hypocrisy were the order of the day. I felt suckered. I wasn't alone.

Betraying the Beatitudes

Here I will skate out on thin ice. Being no believer, I am in no position to lecture Christians on Christianity. Yet I am not unique in thinking that white evangelicals' embrace of partisanship, culture war, and bully-worship betrayed their faith. Many prominent evangelicals (and some ex-evangelicals) believe the same thing. Writes Peter Wehner: "In important respects, much of what is distinctive about American evangelicalism has become antithetical to authentic Christianity. What we're dealing with—not in all cases, of course, but in far too many—is political identity and cultural anxieties, anti-intellectualism and ethnic nationalism, resentments and grievances, all dressed up as Christianity."* The late Michael Gerson: "White religious conservatives have joined a political movement defined by an attitude of 'us' vs. 'them,' and dedicated to the rejection and humiliation of social outsiders and outcasts. . . . This view of politics is closer to 'Game of Thrones' than to the Beatitudes."† Russell Moore: "If there is no eternity, then we should just fall into the same old culture-war patterns as the rest of the world. We should find an in-group and justify whatever they do—and we should identify an out-group so we can relentlessly hound them as stupid and wicked. But if there is a heaven and a hell

---

* Peter Wehner, "The Evangelical Church Is Breaking Apart," *The Atlantic*, October 24, 2021.
† Michael Gerson, "Trump Should Fill Christians with Rage. How Come He Doesn't?" *Washington Post*, September 1, 2022.

and a Holy Spirit, then that posture is not just wrongheaded; it's satanic."*

James Alison, a Catholic theologian and priest, provides a clarifying framework for thinking about the choices white conservative Christians have made. Asked by the podcaster and journalist Andrew Sullivan to summarize the teachings of Jesus, he said in 2023 that they could be boiled down to three tenets. "I think the first one would be to not be afraid. . . . The second one would be, imitate me [i.e., Jesus]. And the third one would be, forgive each other, because that's how you'll be forgiven. That's it."

Don't be afraid. Imitate Jesus. Forgive each other. I am in no position to judge whether those are *the* essential elements of Christianity, but they certainly command broad and deep reverence in America's Christian traditions. In any case, they are the elements of Christianity which resonate most with me, the unbeliever, and which strike me as being (along with the concept of grace) Christianity's distinctive and transcendent moral innovations. So shall we run down the list?

Don't be afraid is one of the Bible's most frequently repeated commands. Yet today's white evangelical world seems consumed by fear. There is fear of the left: "Fear," as Paul Matzko has said, "that if Donald Trump doesn't win in 2016, isn't re-elected in 2020, that is the end of American Christianity as we know it, that the godless humanists and feminists and civil rights activists are going to swamp America and destroy what makes us great." There is fear of cultural change. More than three-fourths of white evangelicals say the country is in danger of losing its identity and culture—by which they mean *their* identity and culture. There is fear that Christians already face

---

* Russell Moore, "We Lose Culture Wars by Putting Them on Trial," *Christianity Today,* March 16, 2023.

discrimination and will soon lose the freedom to practice their faith (many, during Covid, believed they had lost their freedom already). There is fear of demographic change, and with it, ethnic or racial marginalization. A senior pastor in North Carolina, speaking to me about Trump, said, "I believe he spoke to scared white people: *If we're not careful, they're going to take over. Demographically, there's going to be more of them than of us.* For some folks, that's threatening."

Above all, there is fear of loss of status. "They realize they no longer have numbers on their side," Kristin Du Mez told me. "They see that the democratic process will not secure their aims for them. *We've lost the culture; they're coming for us; we've got to defend the right to live as obedient, faithful Christians.*"

My understanding of Christianity and of its totemic instruction not to be afraid is that the Christian's eyes should focus on the next world, not this world; and that, although fear is natural, faith is *super*natural, so that the prospect of redemption in the next world should assuage our fears in this one. "Apocalyptic and hysterical rhetoric is inappropriate for people who are children of the King," James Forsyth, the senior pastor at Cedar Springs Presbyterian Church, told Michael Gerson and Peter Wehner in a 2015 article for *Christianity Today*. "Christians should not be characterized by white knuckles of fear and terror." Sharp Christianity, by contrast, is *literally* a Church of Fear.

Imitating Jesus is something that many evangelicals, including many culture warriors, often do admirably in their capacities as friends, family members, churchgoers, and local volunteers. The west Texas pastor who complained of his congregants' battlefield mindset told me his parishioners generously help the needy who are in their line of sight. "But so much of the Gospel message is to love the marginalized, love the foreigner; and that falls on deaf ears."

Still farther from the personal line of sight is the realm of politics, and there a new wall of separation has arisen: not between church and state, but between personal Christianity and public Christianity. It rationalizes political conduct whose cruelty Christians would abhor in their church lives; it sets up two incommensurable moralities, an absolute one in the personal realm and an instrumental one in the political realm.

Many Christian activists and theologians maintain that Christianity is a seamless garment. It does not accept a distinction between the values Christians display in their personal lives and those they display in their public and political lives. It rejects the attitude which David French, speaking at a Trinity Forum event in 2023, described piquantly as: *I know I'm a bit of an asshole on Twitter, but you should see me in the soup kitchen.* "That's just not the way it works," he said. "You can't cabin off parts of your life. . . . If we wall [civic life] off . . . , we are not exhibiting the virtues that Christ asked us to exhibit."

Nor, he and others add, does Christianity accept that the command to imitate Jesus is conditioned on worldly success: on Christian behavior's succeeding or "working," whatever that means. In a speech to an audience of young conservatives in 2021, Donald Trump, Jr., said this: "We've turned the other cheek, and I understand, sort of, the biblical reference—I understand the mentality—but it's gotten us nothing. Okay? It's gotten us nothing, while we've ceded ground in every major institution in our country." One wonders what exactly Jesus "got" in exchange for being tortured, mutilated, and crucified. David French's comment is worth quoting at length (from the Trinity Forum event, lightly edited for continuity):

> God did not give us a spirit of fear but a power of love and of sound mind. So if you're confronting the world and you're not fearful, but you have confidence in the

power of God, you're loving your neighbor, and you're approaching the world with a sober, sound mind, you're blazing forth in a countercultural way. And what's really important about these obligations: they're not contingent upon *working*. It's not, *You're humble until humility doesn't work.* None of that is contingent. The fruits of the spirit are not just tactics to be deployed to win people over. They're the markers of *Who. We. Are.*

Walling off public from private Christianity in order to "win" (whatever that means) often does *not* win, of course. It blackens the reputation of the faith and fuels justified cynicism about the faithful. More than that, it indentures Jesus Christ to Niccolò Machiavelli, the master of *realpolitik*. Russell Moore recounted, on his podcast:

> So much of this is just tribal signaling. Whose side are you on, and that means who's the common enemy? In almost every arena, when somebody would say, "Wait a minute, let's hold onto and maintain our democratic norms in the political arena," . . . the response would often be, "Get real!" And so it was this sense that if you're not Machiavellian and you're not willing to knife your way through, then you're not living in the real world. That's a point of view, but it's completely opposite to the point of view of Jesus. It's a social Darwinian view. It's not that we ended up with this sort of Joel Osteen prosperity gospel, but we ended up with a depravity gospel.

Forgiving each other as God has forgiven us, and letting God settle our accounts, is the beating heart of Jesus's ministry; of late, though, white evangelicals have not been in a very forgiving mood. In 2023, Trump told a thrilled conservative audience, "I am your warrior. I am your justice. And for those who have been wronged and betrayed: *I am your retribution.*" One might ask: is this doctrine not a root-and-branch repudiation of the ministry of Jesus? If Christians have given their hearts over to "retribution," have they not become antagonists of the creed they claim to follow? Don't they sound an awful lot like the mob who brayed for Jesus's execution?

Can we really, then, blame the secular world for the path conservative Christians have chosen? Or should we rather say that white evangelical Christianity, in its embrace of MAGA values, has repudiated itself? If so, can we expect the secular world not to notice? Russell Moore told the Trinity Forum, "The frantic rage we can often display in supposedly protecting Christian values might feel like strength, but the world sees it for what it is: fear, anxiety, and lack of confidence. They can also see that it's nothing like the confident tranquility of Jesus." Can we blame secular liberalism if so many Americans, especially younger ones, recoil from the Church of Fear? "That sense of paralyzing fear can also fuel the loss of the next generation," Moore writes. "If the only choices we offer are secularization and paganization, we shouldn't be surprised that they choose one or the other."*

And can we blame the secular world for losing confidence in Christianity if so many *Christians* have lost confidence in Christianity? Moore, again, elaborates:

> The church is bleeding out the next generation, not because "the culture" is so opposed to the church's fidelity to the truth, but just the reverse. The culture often does not reject us because they don't believe the church's doc-

* Russell Moore, "Tucker Carlson and the Fear of Being Replaced," *Christianity Today,* May 4, 2023.

trinal and moral teachings, but because they have evidence that the *church* doesn't believe its own doctrinal and
moral teachings. They suspect that Jesus is just a means
to an end—to some political agenda, to a market for sell-
ing merchandise, or for the predatory appetites of some
maniacal narcissist.*

    The pastors I interviewed are not, admittedly, a represen-
tative sample. Still, I found it meaningful that they were not
inclined to blame outside forces for the secularization and "battlefield mindset" they see in their congregations. They acknowledged challenges like social media and cable news and online
pornography; but, like Moore, they were unsparing in their
assessment that the church has failed to stand its ground. One
Southern Baptist pastor told me that the next great mission
field is not abroad or among nonbelievers but within the American evangelical church itself. It needs to be reconverted, he
said, to the message of the gospel.

    We liberals need to wish him well with that mission and
help when we can. We need to try to be part of the solution
rather than the problem—and, I will argue, we can and should
do better on that score. Ultimately, however, we did not cause
Christianity's crisis, and we cannot resolve it. When post-liberals blame secular culture for the decline of Christian values
and look to "revolutionary reforms" and "regime change" for
answers, their daydreaming does the church no favors.

    But perhaps that's enough of my lecturing Christians about
their faith. My business is the salvation of our democracy, not

* Russell Moore, "Enraged by Ravi (Part 1): The Wreckage of Ravi Zacha-
rias," February 15, 2021, available at www.russellmoore.com/2021/02/15/en
raged-by-ravi-part-1-the-wreckage-of-ravi-zacharias/.

of the church. And so I turn to another point: the Church of Fear is as toxic to democracy as it is to Christianity.

What, If Anything, Is Christian Nationalism?

The Church of Fear is not shy about propounding its politics. It wants us to know how it sees the world, and the picture it paints is dire.

   In July 2023, Jim Garlow, the former pastor of Skyline Church near San Diego and a well-known figure in conservative evangelical circles, participated in an onstage conversation at Cornerstone Chapel, a church in Northern Virginia. Garlow is a global activist and unashamed advocate of preaching politics from the pulpit. Asked for a tour d'horizon of "what the enemy is up to," he laid it all out in under an hour.*

   "*Blessed is the nation whose god is the Lord,*" he begins. "Assuming that's true, which it is, then the flip side [is] *Cursed is the nation whose god is not the Lord.*" Therefore we must lift up godly leaders. No government leader is perfect, he cautions, "but I want you to pray for people who are willing to adhere to biblical principles."

   Who might those leaders be? First on his list is President Abdel Fattah el-Sisi of Egypt, "who's holding the Muslim Brotherhood down and rebuilding the Christian churches that the Muslim Brotherhood burns down." (Sisi is an autocrat. Egypt is rated "not free" by Freedom House, which cites, among many examples of the government's authoritarianism, its imprisonment of dissidents in filthy prisons where some are reportedly tortured.) Garlow also is "really applauding" Israeli President

---

* Jim Garlow, interview with Pastor Gary Hamrick, July 19, 2023, available at www.youtube.com/watch?v=9YhBt-LoNv4.

Benjamin Netanyahu for his "badly needed" effort to strip the
Israeli Supreme Court of its power to restrain legislative ma-
jorities. (That effort resulted in massive protests by citizens fearing, with reason, the end of any check on government power.)
Garlow speaks glowingly of his two meetings with Brazil's former president Jair Bolsonaro, who is "falsely charged" with cor-
ruption. (Though Freedom House rated Bolsonaro's Brazil as
free, it notes that his authoritarian tactics included harassing
journalists and threatening the Supreme Court.) And he waxes
enthusiastic over Viktor Orbán, "controversial to some, not to
me. He's giving godly leadership in spite of the accusations
against that man." (Once a success story for post-Soviet democracy, Hungary is now rated only "partly free" by Freedom
House. Orbán's ruling party "pushed through constitutional and
legal changes that have allowed it to consolidate control over
the country's independent institutions, including the judiciary.
The Fidesz government has since passed anti-immigrant and
anti-LGBT+ policies, as well as laws that hamper the operations
of opposition groups, journalists, universities, and nongovern-
mental organizations that are critical of the ruling party.")

What do those leaders have in common (besides their
authoritarian tendencies, that is)? They are "trying to bring the
Judeo-Christian value structure to the country." Also, they are
persecuted. "That's a pattern globally we have run into over and
over: when good people get thrown out, this kind of thing happens," Garlow observes. "Where have we ever seen this pattern
before? . . . We recognize that pattern. I served on President
Trump's faith advisory board."

Meanwhile, the Enemy is on the march. "In one country
after another they use the same language over and over. Satan
is not particularly creative in the way he's operating right now."
Some may be unaware of the stakes because the media obscures
them. ("You need to be very careful and not believe much of

what is reported in media.") Those stakes? "We're up against a cosmic struggle. This is a totalitarian authoritarianism on the move globally. When you talk about World Economic Forum. When you talk about DEI. Or ESGs. Or the fifteen-minute city, if you've heard of that. . . . It goes on and on, the totalitarianism. It's been on a mushroom the last three and a half years at a staggering pace. That's what we're dealing with."*

And don't assume you can hide. You can't. "I assure you, the Enemy would love to take *this* congregation out."

Fortunately, there is something you *can* do. "The issue," Garlow continues, "is, *Can we save the republic? Is America worth saving?* Yes. . . . What's the answer? Biblical truth. So you can take your camera out, you can take your phone out, take a picture of that [QR code] right now and you can order online, or at the table we have a bunch of books for you we've shipped out here." You can get two copies for the price of one! Better yet, buy a whole box for $150 (and don't worry, the author isn't taking a profit).

More good news; Pastor Garlow has another book coming out! It tackles "the biblical foundation for AI. . . . Genetic mutation. Cloning. Reparations. ESG. DEI. BLM. CRT. All of these hot-button topics that you see in the news every night, 60 of them, I lay out the biblical foundations for every one of those. And they're short chapters. They're intentionally very short."

But wait, there's even more! Garlow hopes to make available "a youth version, a children's version, and, if we can, a children's coloring book. The left, the Enemy, is going after people this young, so so are we."

I sell books at my talks (or try to), and mine cost more

---

* "Fifteen-minute cities" may refer to an urban design concept which seeks to make goods and services conveniently accessible on foot and by bike.

than Pastor Garlow's (sorry, you can't get a crate for $150), so
I probably shouldn't tease him for telling audiences they can
save the Republic by buying his book. Still, his short talk dis-
tills so many themes of the Church of Fear that one could write
a dissertation on it. *Christian nationalism:* God smiles only on
Christian countries. *Authoritarianism:* what's a little repression
or torture in pursuit of biblical ends? *Paranoia:* we're always
persecuted. *Apocalypticism:* the whole country—no, the whole
world—is at stake, right at this moment. *Fear:* they're coming
to get you, right here in this church. *Politicization:* every Christian, even young children, must be enlisted in the culture war!

Christian nationalism is deservedly a subject of much
concern nowadays. I confess that, having read a good deal
about it, I have trouble putting my finger on exactly what it
is. Even its nomenclature is contested; David Gushee, for example, makes a persuasive case that the term *authoritarian reactionary Christianity* is more accurate and inclusive. However
named, it does not appear to have a clear or consistent doctrine.
Rather, it seems to involve a cluster of beliefs and characteristics, not all of which occur in every variant or individual. One
element is some form of white nationalism or replacement
theory, the belief that the American way of life is threatened by
people from outside the pale of Christian civilization: minorities, immigrants, Jews, or some other group or movement to
whom America does not properly "belong." The flip side is the
belief that white Christians are the most persecuted group in
America. Instead of being persecuted (in this view), Christianity should be privileged by law and society, or at least should
be first among equals in America's political and cultural life.
And Christians—meaning white, conservative Christians—deserve to win in politics, and they *would* win if the system weren't
rigged.

Students of the subject emphasize that Christian nationalism, whatever it is, is a political phenomenon, not a religious one. Russell Moore says it "refers to the use of Christian words, symbols, or rituals as a means to shore up an ethnic or national identity." Kristin Du Mez identifies it as "the belief that America is God's chosen nation and must be defended as such." Jemar Tisby calls it "an ethno-cultural ideology that uses Christian symbolism to create a permission structure for the acquisition of political power and social control." What all these scholars agree upon is that Christian nationalism is about *power*—not spiritual but worldly. "Those Americans who adhere most strongly to Christian nationalist ideals have *political* interests particularly in mind," write Andrew L. Whitehead and Samuel L. Perry in *Taking America Back for God: Christian Nationalism in the United States*. "Religious interests rank second, if they rank at all." A commitment to Christian nationalism, they add, "is not in any way similar to 'religious commitment' as sociologists often conceptualize it. This is not merely semantics. . . . Christian nationalism often influences Americans' opinions and behaviors in the *exact opposite direction* than traditional religious commitment does."

Who are the adherents, and how many are they? Again, this is hard to pin down. In a 2023 report, the Public Religion Research Institute sought to identify and count both hard-core adherents and softer sympathizers using a screen of five questions, such as whether respondents believe that "the U.S. government should declare America a Christian nation" or that "if the U.S. moves away from our Christian foundations, we will not have a country anymore." They found that about 29 percent of the public is committed to those ideas or sympathizes with them. That was broadly consistent with a separate estimate by Whitehead and Perry.

Two further points are of concern here. One is the association between Christian nationalism, white evangelicalism,

Republican partisanship, and support for Donald Trump and the MAGA movement. In its 2023 report, the Public Religion Research Institute found that most Republicans were Christian nationalist adherents or sympathizers, that most Christian nationalists were white evangelical Protestants, and that most supported Trump. Christian nationalists were also much more likely to express comfort with authoritarianism and political violence. In their affinity for this cluster of political values, Robert P. Jones (who leads the Public Religion Research Institute) has said, "White evangelical Protestants really do stand alone."*

Remember, though, that Christian nationalism is not a religious creed but a political one—which explains why its influence extends beyond the pews to the Republican Party's conservative base more broadly. According to Whitehead and Perry, it "motivates Americans—*whether they are evangelical or not*—to see Trump as the defender of the power and values they perceive are being threatened" (my italics). It is a form of secularization in which Christian identity, partisanship, and MAGA-style ideology swap genes and hybridize to create a kind of pseudo-Christian chimera. In his deeply researched 2023 book *The Godless Crusade,* the Oxford University scholar Tobias Cremer describes an international phenomenon:

> Rather than embracing Christianity as a faith, right-wing populists in the United States, Germany and France are politicizing Christianity as a secularized identity marker to mobilize voters in the context of a new social cleavage, centered around the question of identity and around a

* See Robert P. Jones, public discussion at the Brookings Institution, February 8, 2023, available at www.youtube.com/live/rZLpF-w8-lE.

new wave of right-wing identity politics. In this context, national populists often paint themselves as staunch defenders of the Christian West, while remaining distanced from Christian beliefs, values and institutions. In fact, national populist movements seem to have capitalized on the accelerating secularization of the white working class by openly combining ethnocultural references to Christian heritage and symbols (rather than Christian beliefs) with secular policy stances on issues like immigration, church-state relations, and religious freedom. These developments suggest a significant political shift in Western societies, where the old faith-driven religious right is gradually being replaced by a new identitarian and populist right that is much more secular in nature and may—through its culturalized uses of Christian symbols— be not just a symptom but also a harbinger of secularization. . . . Rather than being dominated by religiously defined culture wars, the new right is increasingly driven by a more secular but no less radical identitarian struggle for Western Civilization: a godless crusade in which Christianity is turned into a secularized "Christianism," an ethno-cultural identifier of the nation and a symbol of whiteness that is increasingly independent of Christian practice, beliefs and the institution of the church.

As Cremer's analysis implies, a second point of concern is this group's tenuous attachment to liberal pluralism—and its influence in the Republican Party. A survey in 2022 by the pollsters Shibley Telhami of the University of Maryland and Stella Rouse of Arizona State University showed that 61 percent of Republicans, and 78 percent of Republican evangelicals, support declaring the United States a Christian nation—even though most acknowledged that doing so would violate the Constitution.*

Jesus and James (Madison)

One should not exaggerate the dangers of Christian nationalism. Its hard-core versions don't have wide support, and polls like the ones I have cited, which test attitudes about abstract claims, can be over-interpreted to sweep in millions of Americans who are not temperamentally or ideologically extreme. Dwelling too much on Christian nationalism may overshadow the bigger concern, which is that Sharp Christianity—the partisan, polarized, fearful style of Christianity I am concerned with here—is inimical to liberal democracy not because it is too nationalistic but because it is insufficiently Christian.

Consider again James Alison's three pillars of Christianity: *don't be afraid; imitate Jesus; forgive each other.* They all have close parallels in liberalism's core civic values.

Don't be afraid. The injunction not to be fearful is a marvelous Christian innovation, not just theologically but also psychologically. "Fear is a powerful drug," the philosopher and psychologist David Livingstone Smith has said. "We respond to fear much more than we respond to love or compassion."† Jesus and Paul understood that if you make people scared enough, you can get them to do anything, including things

*Shibley Telhami and Stella Rouse, *Study of U.S. Public Views on the Ukraine War and on Race, Ethnicity, and Religion,* University of Maryland Critical Issues Poll Study No. 10, undated. See also Rouse and Telhami, "Most Republicans Support Declaring the United States a Christian Nation," *Politico Magazine,* September 21, 2022.

†David Livingstone Smith, podcast conversation with Stephen Bradford Long, July 14, 2023, available at stephenbradfordlong.com/2023/07/14/sacred-tension-making-monsters-david-livingstone-smith/.

which are depraved and self-defeating; but if your faith helps you to focus on what is lasting and important, you will make wiser and more ethical choices. Sharp Christianity whips up exactly the kind of perpetual paranoia which Jesus so inspiringly renounced. "Fear," writes the journalist and former evangelical Jon Ward in his memoir *Testimony: Inside the Evangelical Movement That Failed a Generation,* "drove us to withdraw and retreat from dialogue and cooperation with others who were not like-minded. Fear would drive us to abandon our principles, to seek safety and protection at almost any cost, no matter who it hurt or how it reflected on our faith."

Liberal democracy, too, must guard against fear. Though realistic about human flaws (as Madison wrote: "If men were angels, no government would be necessary"), liberalism relies, more than any other system, on trust: in institutions, in individuals, in rules. Demagogues and tyrants know this, which is why their first step in destroying democracy is to whip up fear: of subversives, foreigners, Jews, Muslims, homosexuals, immigrants, the left, the right, the other political party—whatever works. No one who understands the demagogic value of fear was surprised when Trump began his presidency with a paranoid screed against "American carnage" and ended it by inciting the very mayhem he had foretold.

Liberalism requires us to share power and sometimes relinquish it. It requires us to keep faith with the Constitution even when we aren't winning. It thus requires us to overcome our political fears and approach politics in a spirit of courageous mutuality. The Church of Fear does the opposite. It adheres to political apocalypticism: every election is "Flight 93," a last stand against an existential threat. If the other side wins, then America ceases to be America, and the very survival of Christian witness is in the balance. One pastor I talked to said, "Threat is the dominant relationship with the world outside.

The world is dangerous and threatening, therefore we must defend ourselves. A lot of what I see is the same sort of toxic political vision that I see in other communities, and I want something different for the Christian church." Because it militates against trust and instills hysteria, the Church of Fear is every bit as toxic to democratic civic life as it is to Christianity.

Imitate Jesus. For all the blots on Christendom's historical record, the example of Jesus planted a seed without which liberalism might not have blossomed. With his concern for the downtrodden and his contempt for status and power (including, ultimately, his own), Jesus taught that humans have equal intrinsic worth. In God's eyes, all men and women are precious as ends in themselves, never merely useful as objects for manipulation.

Liberalism embodies these same principles of intrinsic moral worth and equality. Even in extremis, it draws back from measures like torture, enslavement, ethnic cleansing, caste distinctions, and racial discrimination—measures which were standard procedures until liberalism came along. Recall the foundational injunction of Immanuel Kant, liberalism's greatest ethicist: "Act so as to treat humanity, whether in your own person or in that of another, at all times also as an end, and not only as a means." His categorical imperative requires all of us, great and small, to live under the rules we set for others. Adam Smith, in his *Theory of Moral Sentiments,* grounds morality in what he calls *sympathy,* a conscientious effort to put ourselves in others' shoes and have moral empathy for them before making choices which might affect them. In its ethics, liberal morality echoes Jesus: "As you did it to one of the least of these my brethren, you did it to me."

Perhaps the most disturbing thing I have heard from evangelical pastors is that their politicized parishioners put *winning*—or at least *fighting*—ahead of imitating Jesus. As my west Texas pastor friend said, "Everyone says the ends justify the means, but the means are really important." Another pastor told me, "There's this sense that ends justify means, and less faith in the norms of a constitutional democracy as something worth protecting and defending even if it means they might not always win on policy." The battlefield mindset is as toxic to democracy as it is to Christianity.

Forgive each other. "Father," said Jesus, "forgive them; for they know not what they do." Even in childhood, I thought it was amazing that Jesus asked forgiveness for his tormenters, though they had done nothing to deserve it. I understood that building an entire moral system on forgiveness—on *undeserved* forgiveness, what Christians call *grace*—was a radical, visionary, transformational idea.

Liberalism has core ideas which, while not the same as forgiveness and grace, map onto them: *forbearance, civility,* and *compromise.* Forbearance (perhaps the most undervalued of the liberal virtues) requires that when we win in politics, we resist the temptation to drive our adversaries out of public life. We do not strip them of their lives, their votes, their voices, their livings, or their social positions—all of which illiberal regimes do routinely. We forbear because we know they may someday have power over us; but more importantly because they are our fellow citizens, our civic brethren. This was the spirit Lincoln invoked in his first inaugural address, when he said, "We are not enemies, but friends. We must not be enemies. Though passion may have strained, it must not break our bonds of affection." He understood that when politics becomes war, constitutional democracy dies.

Civility is important for the same reason—meaning not just being polite but resolving to hear out our political opponents and treat them as we would wish to be treated. As Alexandra Hudson writes in her 2023 book *The Soul of Civility,* "Civility is a disposition, a way of seeing others as beings endowed with dignity and inherently valuable," a way of conduct which "sees other persons as our moral equals and worthy of basic respect."

And, of course, there is compromise: the essential purpose of the Constitution itself. Liberal regimes reject domination and embrace *negotiation*. The Constitution enshrines a permanent negotiation between branches of government, levels of government, and factions; no one accomplishes much without compromising, and that's the whole point. As I have argued elsewhere, compromise is not just the splitting of differences; it is a dynamic, creative force in its own right, constantly recruiting new voices and ideas to break deadlocks and solve problems. In a liberal democracy, nothing else works without it.*

The Constitution cannot ask us to forgive each other, much less to show grace; but asking us to practice forbearance, civility, and compromise has much the same effect. When Christians take up a spirit of grievance and vengeance, they take aim at liberal democracy. When a pastor calls on Christians to "quit being passive and start being aggressive" and "to fight fire with fire"—and when a theologian declares, "No longer will being nice and relevant cut it"—they are not speaking the language of Jesus *or* of James Madison.

Because Sharp Christianity betrays those three tenets, *don't be afraid, imitate Jesus,* and *forgive each other,* it is un-Christian, and because it is un-Christian in those respects, it is also illiberal. It is not merely in tension with healthy democratic values; it actively undermines them. When American Christians throw in their lot with the MAGA movement, they are joining a movement which was very accurately described

---

* See Jonathan Rauch, "Rescuing Compromise," *National Affairs,* Fall 2013.

(by President Joe Biden) as *semi-fascist*. True, MAGA lacks certain characteristic elements of twentieth-century European-style fascism: militarism, totalism, explicit racism and anti-semitism. Yet there are many other elements of fascism which MAGA emulates. Rejection of elections? *Check.* Contempt for law? *Check.* Corrupt use of government power? *Check.* Nostalgia for purer, simpler times? *Check.* Populist attacks on "enemies of the people"? *Check.* Hostility to the free press? *Check.* Fear of a cosmopolitan, globally subversive left? *Check.* Fear of ethnic and cultural "replacement"? *Check.* Race-baiting and immigrant-bashing? *Check.* Extreme nationalism? *Check.* Cult of masculinity? *Check.* Cult of personality? *Check.* Bully-worship? *Check.* Admiration for authoritarians? *Check.* Violent and dehumanizing rhetoric? *Check.* Threats, harassment, intimidation? *Check.* Militia and street thugs? *Check.* MAGA may not be the full Mussolini, but it gets at least halfway there.

In other countries, we have seen again and again how bad the results can be when authoritarian politicians co-opt conservative churches. Think Italy, Germany, Russia. America is not immune. Mediated through the likes of MAGA, Christianity's crisis of spiritual formation becomes democracy's crisis of civic formation.

A Crisis of Authority

Spiritual formation is a term I had not encountered before starting work on this book. But I soon found I couldn't turn a corner without bumping into it. Very often, it was conjoined with the word *crisis*. As one pastor I interviewed said, "I think it's a spiritual formation crisis. Secular influences are spiritually forming Christians." Andrew Hanauer, an evangelical convert who leads the One America Movement, a faith-based nonprofit, told me, "The fundamental challenge in Christian parlance is of spiritual formation." When I asked him to explain, he replied that we are all formed morally and spiritually by something, and for Christians that something is supposed to be the Bible. "Pastors describe that, more and more, their congregants are formed by a political and cultural view and then hold the church up against that."

As I emphasized earlier, the problem is not that conservative Christians have turned mean or ungenerous in their personal lives. In a podcast, Jon Ward drew an important distinction. "One of the conclusions I've come to . . . is that a lot of the evangelical churches do a pretty good job of discipling their members in private character and private virtue within the family. . . . Broadly, evangelicals are virtuous people in their homes and in their local communities. But they have not been discipled in how to exercise *public* character or *public* virtue."*

I spoke earlier of a new wall of separation, a discontinuity between Christians' personal and political behavior. That is what Ward means by the failure of discipleship in public character; it is what David French and other Christians are getting at when they bemoan Christians' failure to show the humility and kindness on social media and in politics which they practice in their church lives. It is what the Christian writer and activist Michael Wear is getting at when he writes, in his 2024 book *The Spirit of Our Politics: Spiritual Formation and the Renovation of Public Life,* that "our culture, our churches, and many, many individuals—Christians and others—have a view of a domesticated, personalized, and privatized Jesus who is simply not up to the task of our greatest public challenges. We,

*Jon Ward, "Paul D. Miller Untangles the Confusion around Christian Nationalism," October 28, 2022, available at toppodcast.com/podcast_feeds /the-long-game/.

as individuals and as a culture, often do not trust that Christianity has credible resources that are valuable for our public and political lives. We take great pride in our doctrinal acumen, our 'high view' of this or that, while we act as practical atheists in our public life."

As I have said before, secular liberalism and Christianity have separate purposes. They do not need to *ally* (and should not); but they do need to *align,* at least well enough so that democracy's wheels don't come off. Secular liberals cannot expect pastors to deliver civics lectures from the pulpit; in fact, too many pulpits are too politicized already. But we *can* expect the church to disciple its flock in those core Christian teachings which also undergird our democracy. Even accepting that Christianity's accountability is to God, not the U.S. Constitution, we are still obliged to ask: what does *God* think is Christianity's relationship to the Constitution? And it is fair for us to point out that Jesus's teachings have some direct implications on this score.

In that respect, we seculars are entitled to hold the church accountable to the democracy of which it is part. We are entitled to hold it accountable for the choices it makes. While the church's relationship with God is its own business, secular Americans are justified in reminding our Christian friends that the Church of Fear is toxic for them and for us. We are not out of our lane to suggest that what Russell Moore calls "confident Christianity"—which "constantly reminds us that this life is less important than the next [and] demonstrates something of what it means to forgive and serve one another"—needs repair for all our sakes.* In short, we have standing to hope, perhaps even insist, that Christians get their act together.

* Moore, "When the South Loosens Its Bible Belt."

In doing so, we are not asking Christianity to be anything other than itself. We are asking that it eschew fear, imitate Jesus, and forgive—thereby keeping its commitments to God *and* liberal democracy. Michael Wear makes this point eloquently: "The Christian's responsibility for our politics is special, but not because Christians are or should be privileged by law or because America is a 'Christian nation.' For too long, Christians have asserted special status for this country, all while avoiding special responsibility. We share with our fellow citizens—Christians and others—the responsibility in and for our politics in the eyes of the law. Yet Christians are also called by God to be a blessing to the cities and nations in which we've been placed."

Can the church meet that calling? These days, when the Church of Fear seems so strong, pessimism abounds. In *Christianity's American Fate,* David Hollinger passes a gloomy judgment on the evangelical church's relationship with democracy. "Christianity," he writes, "has become an instrument for the most politically, culturally, and theologically reactionary Americans. By any measure, evangelical Protestant leaders have done much more than overzealous progressives to create and shape today's crisis of democracy."

Yet I am not sure that evangelical Protestant *leaders,* whatever their mistakes in the past, are the main problem today. Though some have a lot to answer for, Sharp Christianity appears to be primarily a crisis of followership. Politicization seems to be flowing from the pews to the pulpit more than the other way around. All the pastors I spoke with are unhappy with the partisan tensions and eruptions they see in their churches. Still less are they comfortable with the ebbing of their spiritual authority. They feel dragged along. As one told me, "Pastors are being taken off guard by how politically polarized and radicalized some members of their congregations are. The majority are surprised by it."

The crisis of spiritual formation is foremost a crisis of pastoral authority, not of pastoral influence. As Kristin Du Mez told me, "Many leaders have been rudely awakened to the limits of their own influence, their own power, in their own churches. They thought they could open scripture and have influence. They're finding that if their teaching runs counter to right-wing Republican talking points or Fox News or Tucker Carlson, they'll be up against the ropes, not necessarily by their entire church but by a strong faction within their church." Describing the demoralization so many pastors feel, she told me, "It's this feeling of emptiness, that they have no standing if they run up against this political agenda."

Increasingly, in white Protestant America, divisions run *through* churches, not between them. Some churches have split over their political differences; in others, persistent hard-liners drive out the less politicized, possibly including the pastor. Either way, as schisms and purges run their course, the church becomes both sharper and weaker: more politically divisive and less spiritually fulfilling. Both trends endanger liberal democracy.

They are not easy to reverse. The pews, Du Mez points out, are taking cues from politicians and evangelical media— radio, TV, music labels, and publishers which sell the gospel of fear. "They are all politicized," she said. "That's where the money is, and the gatekeepers are watching that very closely. So it's not that if Trump dies, everyone recalibrates and goes in a different direction. You have to undo these whole systems and replace them with something else, and I don't know what that would be."

Well . . . that is a pretty grim scenario. Still, and thankfully, a whole lot of Christians are unhappy with it. We may wonder if dismayed pastors and battle-weary parishioners— the "church within the church"—can find a better path. For there *are* better paths: ones which integrate scriptural teachings and liberal values, which align spiritual formation with civic virtue, and which, far from being pie in the sky, are flourishing right now.

3
Thick Christianity
The Gospel of Compromise
There are many ways to reconcile Jesus with James Madison

In November 2021, an elderly man, thin and with a dignified demeanor leavened by an impish smile, traveled from Salt Lake City to the University of Virginia with an urgent message. Wasting little time on pleasantries, he launched straight into his theme. "I love this country, which I believe was established with the blessings of God. I love its Constitution, whose principles I believe were divinely inspired. I am, therefore, distressed at the way we are handling the national issues that divide us."

In expressing his distress, he was not speaking merely for himself. This was Dallin Oaks, first counselor in the First Presidency of the Church of Jesus Christ of Latter-day Saints. Then almost 90, he had been a successful lawyer, a justice of the Utah state supreme court, and president of Brigham Young University. Called to the First Presidency in 2018, he was next in line to succeed Russell M. Nelson, the church's president and prophet; and he had become the public voice of the church's civic theology.

A civic theology posits that God expects his people to act

in certain ways, and to follow his commandments, not only in our personal lives but in our civic lives. In that respect, it operates in the same space as Christian nationalism—though what Oaks proposed was antithetical to Christian nationalism and far more profound and promising. When I first read the text of his speech, I felt a frisson. Here was something I had been looking for in my own advocacy of religious liberty and liberal pluralism because it elegantly linked the two.

Oaks's brief began where James Madison and the U.S. Constitution also begin: with the inescapable reality of disagreement and faction. "We have always had to work through serious political conflicts," Oaks said, "but today too many approach that task as if their preferred outcome must entirely prevail over all others, even in our pluralistic society. We need to work for a better way—a way to resolve differences without compromising core values."

Liberalism is a permanent process of public negotiation. Oaks argued that religious communities cannot exempt themselves from democratic deliberation; they must participate in it and abide by the results according to "the principle of honoring both divine and mortal laws." In other words, religious liberty is essential, but people of faith cannot simply enjoy it and walk away. It comes with obligations. "Rendering to Caesar in good faith," said Oaks, "requires religious persons and associations to acknowledge what their government does for them and to be faithful in fulfilling the reciprocal responsibilities they owe to the government and their fellow citizens."

But what are those responsibilities, and how are they to be carried out on occasions when God's law and man's law might conflict? Oaks's example was a clash between antidiscrimination laws requiring merchants and adoption agencies to serve same-sex weddings and couples, on the one hand, and, on the other hand, religious businesses and nonprofits whose faith commitments forbid participation in what they see as sin. Some Christians and their legal allies are quick to strike a confrontational posture when a conflict arises—or even when a conflict does *not* arise, as when, not long ago, a website designer sued successfully to refuse service to same-sex weddings despite not having been asked to serve one. Oaks took a different tack. "The Church of Jesus Christ of Latter-day Saints suggests that a way can be found to reconcile divine and human law—through patience, negotiation, and mutual accommodation, without judicial fiat or other official coercion."

In other words, the first order of the day is not to claim supremacy for either religious or secular law, or to declare an existential clash, but to look—together—for ways to mitigate conflict. Oaks cited two examples, one a political negotiation between the church and Congress in the early twentieth century, the second a recent compromise in Utah which I will describe a little later. "The right relationship between religious freedom and nondiscrimination," he said, "is best achieved by respecting each other enough to negotiate in good faith and by caring for each other enough that the freedom and protection we seek is not for ourselves alone." Like Madison, he placed good-faith negotiation at the very center of the Constitution's meaning, quoting another church official who said, "When we use our religious freedom to bring people together in unity and love, we are defending and preserving religious liberty and the Constitution in a most profound way."

Significantly, Oaks argued that seeking unity through patience, negotiation, and mutual accommodation is not merely a stratagem for getting along with others; it is a charge from God. In remarks to the faithful earlier that year at the church's general conference (a semi-annual global gathering), he said, "Being subject to presidents or rulers of course poses no obstacle to our opposing individual laws or policies. It does require that we exercise our influence civilly and peacefully within the framework of our constitutions and applicable laws. On contested issues, we should seek to moderate and unify."

In Church of Jesus Christ of Latter-day Saints scripture, the U.S. Constitution is specifically named as divinely inspired; and in church doctrine, the Constitution's underlying principles were decreed by God not only for Americans but for all God's children. "I see divine inspiration in the vital purpose of the entire Constitution," Oaks told the general conference. "We are to be governed by *law* and not by *individuals,* and our loyalty is to *the Constitution* and its principles and processes, not to any *office holder.* In this way, all persons are to be equal before the law." (Italics are in the original.)

This doctrine places the church under certain obligations. In a speech in Rome in 2022, Oaks said, "Speaking from a religious perspective, I maintain that followers of Jesus Christ have a duty to seek harmony and peace." This duty pertains not just to seeking harmony and peace in one's own church and family and local community; it is a *civic* commandment, a requirement to approach politics and public debate in a particular way. As Oaks wrote in an article in the scholarly journal *Judicature* in 2023, "*We should not expect or seek total dominance for our own positions.*"

Here the italics are mine, because this is more than a tactical injunction to obey the law in order to stay out of jail, and more than "render unto Caesar" boilerplate. Oaks argues for an alignment between God's moral constitution and Madison's political one. Speaking for the church, he sees patience, negotiation, and compromise not as means to some end, to be jettisoned if the results are unsatisfying, but as social and spiritual ends unto themselves. At the risk of exaggerating or oversimplifying (but only a little), one could put what he is saying this way: *Never dominate, always negotiate—because that is God's plan.*

Why is it God's plan? In a moment, I will explore the church's civic theology in more detail, en route to arguing that it has something to teach both Christianity and liberalism. But first, a quick recap of how we arrived in the realm of Latter-day Saint theology.

In the previous chapters, I argued that neither secular liberalism nor religion can independently deliver all the moral goods people require; but American liberalism and American Christianity are pulling apart, largely (though of course not entirely) because of tragically misguided choices made by many white evangelicals. The result is a crisis for both Christianity and democracy.

This chapter considers pathways toward a positive realignment in which the Christian and secular worlds become more mutually supportive, helping each other uphold the Founders' vision instead of drifting apart into mutual incomprehension. I find reason for hope. Influential religious figures have discovered the hole where a biblically based, pro-democratic civic theology should be and are striving to fill it. Some of them are evangelicals, others not; most are Christian, but one could take inspiration from a rabbi I know who has integrated core American texts into his congregation's Torah study (a concept he and his synagogue are bringing to other congregations). But for today's most intellectually complete and pragmatically proven vision of a distinctively scriptural pluralism, we should travel to Utah.

Countercultural Compromises

My awareness of something interesting afoot in the Church of Jesus Christ of Latter-day Saints (as the church now prefers to be called) came in March 2015, with the announcement of what seemed like a miracle in Utah. Seemingly out of nowhere, at a

press conference in Salt Lake City, conservative state legislators, leaders of the state's LGBT rights community, and senior
representatives of the church announced agreement on legislation extending nondiscrimination protections to LGBT Utahns
while also providing targeted exemptions for religious organizations. The bill, SB 296, passed the conservative legislature
with overwhelming support.

Madison put compromise at the heart of the Constitution because he correctly understood compromise to be more
than a mechanical, difference-splitting approach to managing
conflict. While it can sometimes be mere difference-splitting,
compromise is more often a creative, generative, pro-social en-
deavor in its own right. If the parties in a disagreement dead-
lock, they gather more information, bring in new factions and
voices, imagine innovations and workarounds. The result is
often better than what anyone started with. And the legislative
outcome is not the only product; just as important are the relationships built during negotiations, the habits of collaboration formed, and the feelings of goodwill and fellowship which
arise among previously antagonistic groups. Simply by having
to interact and do business, the parties to a negotiation develop the civic habits of peaceful coexistence and unlearn the
habits of domination and distrust.

That happened in Utah. "To me the process here may
be even more important than the legislation," Troy Williams,
the executive director of Equality Utah, the state's main LGBT
group, told me. "When I sit down with folks, I'll never see them
as an enemy or opponent. I'll see them as future ally, even if
we're not there yet." When I asked him to name the downsides
of SB 296 from the point of view of Utah's LGBT community,
he couldn't think of a single one. "The culture has changed here
in Utah," he said. "In every possible way, Utah is now a safer
and more welcoming state for the LGBTQ community." When

I asked if the same change would have happened without SB 296, he replied with a firm no. "It changed the dynamic forever in the legislature. I've watched so many legislators open up their hearts in this process."* Capitalizing on the channels of communication and trust they had built, conservative legislators and Equality Utah were able to collaborate on subsequent hot-button issues such as gay conversion therapy.

The compromise of 2015 did not come out of nowhere. In 2008, the church had gone all-in to back California's Proposition 8, which added a ban on same-sex marriage to the state's constitution (ending a brief period in which same-sex marriage had been legalized by the state's supreme court). The church called upon its members in California to contribute and canvass in support of the initiative; it even had local leaders read a statement over every Latter-day Saint pulpit in California, asking members to "do all you can to support the proposed constitutional amendment by donating of your means and time to assure that marriage in California is legally defined as being between a man and a woman." Although Proposition 8 won at the ballot box, the church's heavy-handed involvement—which may have been decisive—caused an uproar whose fury shocked and chastened the church's leadership. Quietly, the church opened lines of communication with the LGBT community in Utah. Eyebrows went up in 2009 when the church threw its support behind Salt Lake City's ban on anti-gay discrimination in housing and employment. That led to several years of quiet, intense conversations between the church and the LGBT community, initially aimed at listening and learning, then turning more substantive. SB 296 was only the visible tip of a larger, mostly submerged negotiation.

*Jonathan Rauch, "Meeting in the Middle on Religious and LGBTQ Rights," *Deseret News*, May 5, 2021.

I was (and still am) a devoted advocate of both LGBT equality, especially marriage, and religious liberty. I believed there was room and need to negotiate pathways around conflicts. For me, SB 296 was inspirational. And indeed, it inspired similar efforts in other states, as well as negotiations between a center-right LGBT group called the American Unity Fund and a coalition of religious groups (including the Church of Jesus Christ of Latter-day Saints) leading to a proposed federal compromise called the Fairness for All Act. None of those efforts bore fruit—until, unexpectedly, they did.

In 2022, concurring with the Supreme Court's *Dobbs* decision overturning the *Roe v. Wade* abortion ruling, Justice Clarence Thomas included language suggesting that same-sex marriage, legalized by the court in 2015, might be next on the chopping block. In Congress, House Democrats responded with the Respect for Marriage Act, a bill establishing same-sex marriage in federal law. Seeing an opportunity, the Fairness for All coalition in the Senate added some significant religious liberty protections. By strongly stating that the federal government will not treat opposition to same-sex marriage as the equivalent of racism, and that the government will not use federal instruments like contracts and tax breaks to coerce acceptance of same-sex marriage, the bill squarely addressed the religious community's two biggest fears. It passed with bipartisan support—and with the support of the Church of Jesus Christ of Latter-day Saints, which did not endorse the same-sex marriage provisions but worked to get the bill enacted and praised its religious liberty provisions as "historic and commendable."

One needs to step back and appreciate why all this matters. Socially, the teachings of the Church of Jesus Christ of Latter-day Saints are conservative. Marriage is between one man and one woman; homosexuality is a sin, and a person who practices it unrepentantly cannot be a church member. For the most part, conservative Protestants and Catholics who share this view have assumed that America's laws should reflect God's laws. *Reflect* does not mean *copy* or *embody*. But because, for example, the Bible (purportedly) says that homosexuality is an abomination, conservative Christians have supported laws criminalizing consensual homosexual intimacy ("sodomy"). To such conservatives, it makes no sense to oppose same-sex marriage as sinful and unbiblical while supporting a law enshrining that very thing.

One Church of Jesus Christ of Latter-day Saints officer recalled to me a conversation he had with a Roman Catholic archbishop who was perplexed by the church's willingness to compromise on LGBT issues. In its 2019 guide *Forming Consciences for Faithful Citizenship*, the U.S. Conference of Catholic Bishops calls participation in political life "a moral obligation" and emphasizes a long list of policy positions Catholics should support. *Compromise* is mentioned only three times in its 53 pages, and always in a negative context (as in, "We cannot compromise basic principles or moral teaching"). "We should work with others to advance our moral principles," the bishops say, but that injunction is instrumental, a means to an end, not an end in itself. One Catholic commentator told me, "I think that Catholic teaching recognizes that compromise is legitimate on the application of principles to legislation, but the bishops are simply not interested in compromising on these [moral] issues."

It was no surprise, then, that the bishops stridently opposed the Respect for Marriage Act, saying that the church "will always uphold the unique meaning of marriage as a lifelong, exclusive union of one man and one woman." Similarly, Andrew Walker of the Southern Baptist Theological Seminary voiced the prevalent view among evangelicals when he wrote on

Twitter: "Even if the Respect for Marriage Act had incredible religious liberty protections (it doesn't), it still violates a basic principle of moral construction related to public policy: Law should always reflect truth. It is thus wrong to tell a lie about what marriage is." In other words, the only morally acceptable compromise involving same-sex marriage is *no* compromise.

So why was the Church of Jesus Christ of Latter-day Saints defending my legal right to marry a man and, beyond that, endorsing compromise as a good in and of itself? When I asked Dallin Oaks, he acknowledged tactical considerations. "We're doctrinally against it," he told me, meaning same-sex marriage, "but we believe in living under the Constitution and laws of the United States. So we don't think we give up very much by having Congress enact something that's already the law under the Supreme Court, and what we gain in the Respect for Marriage Act as amended is important enough. What we lose by codifying something that already exists is insignificant."

Okay, fair enough. But there had to be more to it than shrewd maneuvering. The church could have sat on the sidelines, saying and doing nothing to help the bill pass, or it could have joined with many other conservative religious groups in demanding protection for religious liberty *without* protection for marriage equality—a purist posture which would have been cost-free. Yet here was the Church of Jesus Christ of Latter-day Saints actively supporting a compromise contravening a core doctrine, when doing so was *not* cost-free.

Oaks, when we spoke about it, was well aware that the church's conciliatory approach is conspicuously countercultural in the conservative religious world. The search for a way in the middle "means we've left some evangelicals behind and we don't have the Catholic support that we usually have, and our position does not track well with conservative Republicans. So there are quite a few points of strain on that." He professed not to care about other churches' reactions ("I'm only concerned about what I said being right"), and he seemed quite cheerful about coloring outside the lines. He told me,

> I have a professional lifetime interest in the Constitution of the United States, and how it could never have been adopted without compromise among groups that feel differently on powerful issues but found a way to realize that if they would give up on things that were less important they could achieve a common goal that's most important of all. I think that's an approach that has become less and less feasible during my lifetime. A different approach seems to be dominant in government and much public thinking, including among many religious people of different denominations. As I've prayerfully pondered and tried to see what God would have us do and what is good for our nation, I came to the position that I expressed in the lecture in Virginia.

Why might God require the Church of Jesus Christ of Latter-day Saints to take an approach which is, by the standards of conservative Christianity, distinctly countercultural, not to mention unpopular and, in the view of many, unbiblical? The answer goes deep.

A Thick and Strong Church

Before approaching that answer, I need to make five prefatory points. The first is that, for all the admiration I will express in the paragraphs which follow, I am by no means a fan of all elements of the church and its theology. I find its teachings about homosexuality, in particular, repugnant and harmful, and its teachings about gender roles discriminatory and archaic. But the depth of our differences is precisely what makes the church's ideas about pluralism so compelling.

The second point is that the Church of Jesus Christ of Latter-day Saints takes conservative views on social issues which resemble those of conservative evangelicals. Moreover, in the United States the two traditions have similar demographic profiles: largely white and disproportionately Republican. Those similarities make it all the more significant that the Church of Jesus Christ of Latter-day Saints has consciously chosen to reject the Church of Fear. Demographics and ideology, it turns out, do not dictate theology. We learn from the Church of Jesus Christ of Latter-day Saints that Christians can *choose* their civic posture. They are not merely buffeted hither and yon by outside cultural winds and secular pressures. They are not necessarily forced into an oppositional, confrontational stance by their conservative views.

A third observation: the Church of Jesus Christ of Latter-day Saints is not a "thin" religion. It has not blended into the cultural zeitgeist or watered down its requirements. Just the opposite; it is one of America's most prominent examples of a *thick* faith, one which is both demanding and enfolding, combining high personal investment with high communal returns. "Let us here observe," said Joseph Smith, the church's founder, "that a religion that does not require the sacrifice of all things never has power sufficient to produce the faith necessary unto life and salvation."

It is instructive to dilate for a moment on just how "thick"—how demanding—the church is. In their high-school years, church members are expected to attend a program of weekday religious instruction called Seminary. (This frequently happens before school, although in Utah and some other places it can be accomplished through released time.) "Young people in the church make a tremendous sacrifice for that," Clark Gilbert, the church's education commissioner, told me, recalling how he used to wake up at 6 a.m. every day. High schoolers are also expected to attend at least one session of a one-week summer camp, which, Gilbert said, focuses in large part on "how do you hang on to your faith in a world that imposes a different perspective on you?" There is also a weekly evening youth program, plus an hour of Sunday school weekly at church. Plus the church encourages nightly scripture study with family. "We're not going to just have the church teach our kids," Gilbert said. "Part of the way adults stay strong is we're expected to teach ourselves and teach at home."

Not every church member does all those things, of course (are there enough hours in the day?), but they do a lot. Referring to the 10,000 hours of training supposedly required for proficiency in a skill or sport, Gilbert said, "We hit the 10,000 hours by the time we graduate high school."

After high school, in university, many go on to additional studies, called Institute, for several hours a week. As they leave their teens, about 40 percent take two years for missionary work, an experience which, in my interviews with them, former missionaries uniformly described as life-changing. Thus prepared, when church members reach the world of work they are called to all kinds of volunteer assignments, ranging from teaching Sunday school to organizing charitable programs. The church relies on lay members to serve as clergy (called bishops), usually for five-year terms. One bishop—a professional with a demanding day job—estimated putting in 15 hours a week at the church, unpaid. Those without a specific calling are expected to volunteer several hours a week, for example by teaching in youth programs or distributing food to the needy.

If I were to single out one aspect as characteristic of the church's "thickness"—its wraparound, high-touch social technology for keeping members committed and connected—I would choose a program the church refers to as *ministering brothers and sisters*. Most church members, perhaps 70 percent, are assigned responsibility, with a partner, to look after a family—one or more of whose members, in turn, will act as ministering brother or sister to another family. Ministering duties are not spelled out specifically, but in normal times the ministering pair would check in with their family once a month or so for a scripture lesson or an update. If there's a crisis, engagement becomes more intense. Gilbert recalls that when his house burned down, the ministering sister showed up at 10 p.m. to help. "In our church," he told me, only half-jokingly, "we assign friends."

I recount all of that by way of giving a feel for the strong demands the church makes, and the strong bonds it creates. Which leads me to a fourth observation: the church is healthy. Vibrant, in fact. Worldwide, it is growing. In the United States, its growth seems to have leveled off after a period of robust expansion. Accurate counts are hard to come by because not all those listed as members on church rolls are active, but in a 2019 study the church demographer Stephen Cranney estimated the rate of attrition in the United States to be more or less offset by the rate of conversion.* This makes a distinct contrast with the shrinkage of the mainline and evangelical denominations.

Finally, despite its misstep in 2008, the church has made a conscious choice not to dabble in partisan politics. It specifically forbids political preaching. The church leadership has rejected pleas, from inside and outside, to involve itself in issues like immigration and the environment. Some members, I was told, itch to see the church wade into the culture wars; but

---

* Stephen Cranney, "Who Is Leaving the Church?" *BYU Studies Quarterly* 58, No. 1 (2019).

church officials I spoke with, including not only higher-ups in Salt Lake City but also ordinary bishops (i.e., local lay pastors), said that if a bishop or other ecclesiastical authority ventured into partisan politics, he would be promptly counseled and corrected. Sunday school and Seminary instruction, which I observed, stick to exposition of the church's four sacred texts, taught on the same weekly schedule around the world, so that a student could move from Maryland to Manila without missing a verse. In the worship services and educational sessions I observed, I saw no hint of politics, even by implication.

Taking those observations together, we may pause to note something meaningful. The Church of Jesus Christ of Latter-day Saints achieved all of what I just mentioned without secularizing; without blending into the surrounding culture; without relinquishing its exacting requirements; and without yielding to demands that it embrace partisan politics and preach the culture wars. True, it has adapted in a variety of ways: obvious examples include banning polygamy and accepting African Americans into the priesthood. (Hope springs eternal for revelations about homosexuality and women.) But no one who even dips a toe in its waters thinks the church has lost its cultural distinctiveness or its theological moorings. To the contrary, the Church of Jesus Christ of Latter-day Saints stands as one of our country's most prominent examples of a thick church—one which demands much of its adherents and offers much back to them.

All of this, taken together, poses quite a problem for "post-liberal" critics of the classical liberal tradition. According to them, it should not be possible for a traditionalist, conservative church to embrace negotiation and mutual accommodation amid today's consumeristic, individualistic, homogenizing culture while also preserving its values and its distinctiveness. If the post-liberal critique were true, the Church of Jesus Christ

of Latter-day Saints should have been assimilated long ago by
the relentlessly liberal Borg. Its members should be clamoring
for a low-maintenance, unchallenging experience, and its leaders should be yielding to the pressures of social media and the
sexual revolution. Resistance is futile, right?

In fact, the church helps us understand why aligning with
liberal pluralism is not part of the problem for American Christianity; it is part of the solution.

"Nits Will Make Lice"

Latter-day Saints' attitudes toward pluralism, law, and religious
freedom date back to the founding of the church. From the
beginning, the church was persecuted, often savagely. Like the
Jews, the Saints were driven from one place to the next by po-
grom and government persecution. Missouri's governor ordered
them expelled from the state or, if need be, "exterminated."
(An original copy of the governor's extermination order is on
display at the church history museum in Salt Lake City. It
makes for a chilling read.) Joseph Smith, the church's founder,
was martyred along with his brother. Many others were killed,
uprooted, and otherwise ethnically cleansed. In the Haun's Mill
massacre, as the University of Utah historian Paul Reeve told
me, three boys attempting to hide were murdered by attackers
who said, in justification, "Nits will make lice."

That history is not ancient: its scars remain. Reeve star-
tled me by mentioning that one of those three murdered boys
was his relative. Dallin Oaks told me that his great aunt, whom
he knew as a boy, was jailed for contempt of court in a polygamy case. Perhaps the most obvious and frequently made point
about the modern church's attitude toward democracy is that
the memory of persecution has bred sensitivity to the importance of religious freedom and pluralism—as well as a com-

pulsion to prevent the Constitution's First Amendment guar-
antee from ever again being traduced as it so egregiously was
in their case.

Joseph Smith's commitment to religious pluralism no
doubt stemmed in part from the persecution he and his followers experienced; yet his writings on the subject transcend
their historical moment, evincing a conviction which seems
spiritual and even visionary. In the eleventh of his thirteen
articles of faith, he says, "We claim the privilege of worshiping
Almighty God according to the dictates of our own conscience,
and allow all men the same privilege, let them worship how,
where, or what they may." And in 1843 he said:

> The Saints can testify whether I am willing to lay down
> my life for my brethren. If it has been demonstrated that
> I have been willing to die for a "Mormon," I am bold to
> declare before Heaven that I am just as ready to die in
> defending the rights of a Presbyterian, a Baptist, or a good
> man of any other denomination; for the same principle
> which would trample upon the rights of the Latter-day
> Saints would trample upon the rights of the Roman Cath-
> olics, or of any other denomination who may be unpop-
> ular and too weak to defend themselves.

In 1843, defending Roman Catholics was not exactly
popular in the United States, but Smith followed his word with
deeds. When the church settled in Nauvoo, Illinois, the city
council, led by mayor Joseph Smith, passed a sweeping religious-
liberty ordinance: "Be it ordained by the City Council of the
city of Nauvoo, that the Catholics, Presbyterians, Methodists,
Baptists, Latter-Day-Saints, Quakers, Episcopalians, Universal-
ists, Unitarians, Mohammedans, and all other religious sects,
and denominations, whatever, shall have free toleration, and

equal privileges, in this city."* Dismayed by the U.S. government's refusal to enforce the church's civil rights, Smith went so far as to commission a Council of Fifty to propose constitutional revisions requiring "the armies of the government" to enforce "principles of liberty" for all people, not just the Protestant majority—and, notes Reeve, in his essay "The Council of Fifty and the Search for Religious Liberty," Smith "included as members of the Council of Fifty those of other faiths or of no faith as an explicit demonstration of his views." Reeve writes:

> For Joseph Smith, it was not enough to merely tolerate people of other faiths or of no faith. Religious bigotry had no place in his worldview. He stated, "God cannot save or damn a man only on the principle that every man acts, chooses and worships for himself; hence the importance of thrusting from us every spirit of bigotry and intolerance toward a mans [sic] religious sentiments, that spirit which has drenched the earth with blood." He called [on] the council to witness that "the principles of intollerance [sic] and bigotry never had a place in this kingdom, nor in my breast, and that he is even then ready to die rather than yield to such things."

Smith even made federal enforcement of religious liberty the central plank of his 1844 presidential candidacy (which triggered the tragic chain of events leading to his murder).

In the modern church, to paraphrase Faulkner, the past is not dead; it's not even the past. When I visited Salt Lake City for interviews with church officials and members, I was ambushed by an unexpected sense of recognition and kinship. As

---

* Not all of the council's actions were liberal; it condemned a dissident newspaper as a public nuisance and destroyed its presses.

a Jew, I grew up immersed in a narrative of persecution, flight, exile, vulnerability, and vigilance. The Latter-day Saints have their own story of flight and exile: according to Smith's revelation, the church's earthly Zion is Jackson County, Missouri, not Salt Lake City. Like the Jews, the Latter-day Saints were driven out of their promised land and their plan for a great temple there is today unfulfilled. I feel an immense pride in America's pluralism and tolerance while remaining conscious—as a Jew and also as a homosexual—of my status as a minority and an outsider. I experience the United States as my own country; yet more (I suspect) than my white Protestant friends, I feel that my sense of belonging to America does not translate into a sense that America belongs to me. I understand exactly what a Latter-day Saint who works in a church education program meant when he said, matter-of-factly, "We get persecuted, but so what?" Religious bigotry remains a fact of life for his church and perhaps always will, but he refuses to be defined by it. (That's how I feel about antisemitism and homophobia.) When he emphasized the importance of looking forward and doing good in the world rather than nursing grievance, I saw a stark contrast with the Church of Fear, which is livid with aggrievement. The Latter-day Saint attitude, like the Jewish attitude, is that we may be blessed with safety and influence here in America, but we can never feel *entitled* to them. We cannot "lose our country" because it is not ours to lose; rather, we are here to share it.

When I asked Dallin Oaks about the influence of the church's history as a persecuted minority, he gave a complicated answer. "That can never escape the consciousness of anyone who knows the church's history of persecution, and most of the church leadership has that in their pedigree charts. You can't escape those memories." But, he added, "to say they motivate the church's position [today] I think is wrong." He said the church looks ahead to the future and its mission of building a global membership. There, again, was the line I heard also from the rank and file: be aware of the past, be informed by it, but do not be defined or aggrieved by it.

A sociologist who maintains that the church's civic posture is shaped by its history would certainly be correct, but only up to a point. To take religion seriously, one must take religious doctrine seriously. One must move from history and sociology to theology. And when one examines the theology of the Church of Jesus Christ of Latter-day Saints, one finds a surprise. The Book of Mormon converges with the Book of Madison.

A Godly Pluralism

Here I am on thin ice again—even thinner than in the last chapter, when I tried to explain Christianity to Christians. I am even more the amateur when it comes to explaining Latter-day Saint doctrine. The case I am about to make leans on the work of Terryl Givens, a respected theologian and intellectual historian of the Church of Jesus Christ of Latter-day Saints. It is buttressed by interviews and conversations with church officials and scholars. But it is not intended to be an authoritative statement of doctrine. Instead, it is an outsider's effort to understand specific aspects of a complex and singular teaching, and to place them within my own secular framework in hopes of learning from them.

In my conversations with leaders and members of the Church of Jesus Christ of Latter-day Saints, the concept of *agency* came up far more often than any other doctrinal idea. "Nothing is quite so core as agency is to Mormonism," Kathleen Flake, a professor of Mormon studies at the University of Virginia, told me. I heard it invoked in all kinds of contexts. For example, when I asked Rusty Bowers, a former speaker of the Arizona state House of Representatives and a member of the Church of Jesus Christ of Latter-day Saints, why he had championed a version of the Utah compromise in Arizona, despite knowing it lacked the votes to pass, he went straight to agency. Church scripture, he told me, "strongly speaks about the absolute necessity of the expression of free conscience. If we believe that, why don't we allow that?" He elaborated that "as children of God we cannot be forced to follow him. It has to be a willful offering of the heart."

What is *agency*, and what does it have to do with legislative politics about LGBT rights in Arizona? Well . . . it begins in the Garden of Eden.

Following the teaching of Saint Augustine and many subsequent saints and sages, most Christians believe that Eve and Adam sinned by defying God's command not to eat the fruit of knowledge, and that the punishment was their expulsion from paradise and humanity's eternal burdens of mortality and original sin. In my Jewish education, I was taught a similar story of Edenic disobedience and punishment, though without the doctrine of original sin. I will confess that, from the time I first heard that interpretation, it has puzzled me. If God had not wanted Eve to eat the fruit, why did he make it available? Why did he also put a tempter in her path? Most fundamentally, I thought, Eve and Adam had made a praiseworthy choice. Humans before the Fall were cattle, nourished and fed but also naked and naïve, without knowledge of good and evil and thus lacking moral sense, humanity's defining trait. How can it be right to choose to be like sheep and cows? Isn't our capacity for moral reasoning a gift, not a curse?

Taking those questions on board, Latter-day Saint theology breaks with the doctrine of original sin. God warned that eating the fruit of knowledge would have grave consequences but deliberately provided the option. Eve's choice to accept those consequences was part of God's plan and therefore not sinful or wicked, but courageous. As Dallin Oaks wrote in 1993, "Some Christians condemn Eve for her act, concluding that she and her daughters are somehow flawed by it. Not the Latter-day Saints! Informed by revelation, we celebrate Eve's act and honor her wisdom and courage in the great episode called the Fall." God gave humans the capacity for moral awareness and choice, and in seizing the opportunity instead of rejecting it, we became more like God. "Humankind and God now share a common moral awareness, a common capacity to judge between right and wrong, a common capacity for love," write Terryl Givens and Fiona Givens in *The God Who Weeps: How Mormonism Makes Sense of Life.* "Instead of deploring Eve's and Adam's transgression, one might find in it a cause for rejoicing."

From the idea that the first couple's decision was not sinful, it follows that there is no original sin. Of course, humans have a *propensity* to sin; life is full of temptations and our own natures tempt and mislead us. But we do not *inherit* sinfulness; we are born innocent. As our lives unfold, we draw closer to God or farther from God through the choices we make. "At Eve's courageous instigation," write the Givenses, she and Adam "opt to lose paradise, hoping to eventually regain heaven—but transformed and ennobled by the schoolhouse of experience that comprises mortality. For this kind of education, nothing short of total immersion in a world of choice and consequence will suffice, and sin is one of those consequences. . . . Only by choosing the good and experiencing its fruit do we learn to savor and embrace the good." We *learn* goodness by confronting choices in the world and choosing well; and in the process of learning goodness, we become more like God.

Now, in some respects, the Latter-day Saints' emphasis on choice sounds like the conventional Christian doctrine of free will. After all, there is no virtue in doing right if we do not also have the ability to do wrong. So is agency just free will under a different name? Not quite. Free will entails the *capacity* to make moral or immoral choices. But in order to learn from life's schooling, we must have more than just the capacity to make moral or immoral choices; *we must also have morally consequential choices to make*—and inevitably, we will make some flawed and even wrong choices. "Moral agency is predicated on a causal connection between choice and consequence," Terryl Givens writes, in *Wrestling the Angel: The Foundations of Mormon Thought.* "Given the freedom to choose, individuals must be granted the fruits of their choices, good or ill, or such freedom would be only a shadow of genuine agency."

The implication, then, is that we are not born guilty, but merely inadequate. We are not fallen but unformed. Life is not a process of moral repair or atonement under the oppressive curse of original sin; it is a process of moral development under the tutelage of experience. And we cannot develop morally unless we confront all kinds of choices, not just pre-approved ones—thus allowing us to exert *agency.* Efforts to protect us from bad choices by restricting agency may be well intentioned, but they deprive us of the opportunity to learn from our errors and inadequacies, stunting our moral development and ultimately thwarting our godlike potential.

Moreover, according to the church, the doctrine of agency applies to all persons, not only members of the Church of Jesus Christ of Latter-day Saints. The doctrine is universal. *Everyone* must be able to make decisions according to the dictates of judgment and conscience. This is our human inheritance from the time of creation. As Joseph Smith taught in a speech in 1840, "I believe that a man is a moral, responsible, free agent."

From here it is but a short step to Madisonian pluralism. "*First,*" writes Oaks in his *Judicature* article, "we learn that God grants us moral agency and, consequently, we are not only free to choose and to act according to our choices, but we are also accountable to God for those choices. *Second,* the most desirable political condition for the exercise of agency is maximum freedom for persons to act personally without tyrannical dictate."

Of course, some choices will come into conflict. We can't exert unfettered agency without sometimes causing harm to others or violating others' agency. The church and the Constitution (a divinely inspired document, remember) prescribe the same remedy. "Where there is genuine conflict, one constitutional right should not be invoked to try to cancel another constitutional right," Oaks said at UVA. "Both need to be balanced legally and negotiated politically in a way that upholds both essential rights to the greatest extent possible."

Note the phrase "balanced legally and negotiated politically." In a diverse society, a sustainable and just balance will not be found abstractly or doctrinally or legalistically, nor will it be found if only one side has a vote. Finding balance requires "patience, negotiation, and mutual accommodation." It requires active political interaction. Which requires, in turn, a particular civic mindset. We now see the theological underpinnings for Oaks's dictum: *We should not expect or seek total dominance for our own positions.* If I impose my will politically to limit your agency, I have deprived you of a pathway toward godliness; and so I have sinned.

Here we have something quite impressive: a fully formed, coherent scriptural foundation for Madisonian pluralism. It is the polar antithesis of Christian nationalism and it rejects and repudiates Christian dominionism. So why might Arizona House speaker Bowers commit himself to compromising on LGBT rights, despite believing that homosexual behavior violates God's law? Why might the church support the Utah compromise and the Respect for Marriage Act? Because those measures protect the church's ability to teach and practice its doctrines about marriage and sexuality within its own institutions, while also protecting, in the larger society, people's ability to make their own choices about marriage and sexuality. Thus can "patience, negotiation, and mutual accommodation" advance religious freedom and personal freedom in tandem, increasing the net sum of agency and advancing the moral development of individuals and society. Which is liberal doctrine in a nutshell!

I am not claiming that the Church of Jesus Christ of Latter-day Saints always endorses libertarian public policies (Utah is one of only two states where all forms of gambling are illegal), or that the church is never hypocritical or domineering. Nor am I claiming that the church's doctrines and practices magically resolve tensions between faith groups and secular society. I *am* arguing that American liberals—and, still more important, American Christians—should pay attention to what the church has laid before us: a civic theology which aligns scriptural and constitutional values, not merely as a matter of expediency but as an intrinsic element of God's plan.

The church here provides as dramatic a contrast as you could imagine with the civic theology of Christian nationalism and its offshoots. It provides an account of Christian citizenship which is not defensive, fearful, or self-isolating, but which embraces the messy, frustrating process of negotiation as bringing Americans closer to God. It renounces as unscriptural the zero-sum, Flight 93 mentality, in which only one side can triumph and everything depends on winning the next election. It rejects any effort to model politics on warfare, any desire to drink the other side's tears. It also rejects the radical version of progressivism which would impose secular law on religious life, regardless of religious practices and objections. Instead, it supports a balanced, negotiated approach in which the two sides meet as equals and make room for each other. In that respect, it provides for accountability to both God and the Constitution.

If you are a secular progressive who wants to withdraw all government grants and contracts from (say) Brigham Young University unless it allows same-sex couples into its married dorms, you will not like this approach. Nor will you like it if you are a post-liberal or Christian nationalist who wants to re-write law to reflect religious principles like Sunday closing or contraceptive bans. But your alternative strategy of trying to dominate or destroy the other side will be less successful and more divisive; and ultimately, your insistence on purism will weaken the social fabric on which your faith's freedom and agency ultimately depend.

Theology Matters

I don't need to be psychic to anticipate the next question. All of that theology is interesting, but is it applicable beyond the Church of Jesus Christ of Latter-day Saints? Can American evangelicals take anything from it? No other church shares the Latter-day Saints' theology, scripture, or hierarchy. When I tried to persuade a Southern Baptist minister that the Fall was a good thing, I didn't get to first base. If evangelicals need to convert to Latter-day Sainthood in order to embrace plural-ism, we're stuck.

Fortunately, one need not replicate the Church of Jesus Christ of Latter-day Saints' theology in order to learn from it. The Latter-day Saints' example allows us to make some hope-ful observations, none of which requires agreement with their theology.

First, it shows that a pluralistic civic theology is possible in America today. The post-liberals are wrong to claim that liberalism is inherently antithetical to conservative and communitarian varieties of Christianity. The Church of Fear is wrong to insist on a divisive, oppositional attitude toward politics. You need not surrender your religious faith or identity in order to embrace Madison's constitutional pluralism. You need not regard compromise as defeat and opponents as enemies. Better still, tearing down the wall of separation between personal and public Christian values strengthens both. Seeking to "moderate and unify" in civic life is both pious and public-spirited.

Second, the church's example also demonstrates that Christian civic pluralism is practical. You can apply it to public policy, get actual deals done, and come out ahead. You can obtain more of what you need through patience, negotiation, and mutual accommodation than by rioting in the Capitol or hollering about Flight 93 elections. While it is true that the fruits of the spirit should not be judged on the basis of whether they "work," they often *do* work. And not just for the Church of Jesus Christ of Latter-day Saints. Others who participated in the negotiations leading to the Fairness for All proposal and the Respect for Marriage Act included the Seventh-day Adventist World Church, the National Association of Evangelicals, the Council for Christian Colleges & Universities, and the (Jewish) Orthodox Union. None of those faith groups supports same-sex marriage as a religious matter or is theologically progressive; but all saw their mission in pluralism, not purism.

Third, while other Christian traditions differ from the Church of Jesus Christ of Latter-day Saints on theological particulars (and, it should be noted, some evangelicals do not regard Latter-day Saints as Christians), a church which makes an effort to notice and foreground the liberal elements of

Christian teaching has plenty to work with. I dwelled on Latter-day Saint teachings about agency and moral development not for their own sake but to demonstrate that the church's theology drives its approach to politics, not the other way around. The church is not compromising or deforming its doctrines to conform with contemporary exigencies; rather, it is teaching and modeling core doctrines which serve God *and* help us live together. And—the operative point—*evangelicals can do this, too.* As I argued in the previous chapter, core tenets of Christianity align with Madisonian pluralism. There are plenty of doctrinal pathways which evangelicals can take to pluralism. In recent years, evangelical illiberalism has been driven not by the dictates of scripture but by ignoring many of those dictates, or applying them selectively and inconsistently. After its Proposition 8 debacle in 2008, the Church of Jesus Christ of Latter-day Saints has foregrounded those elements of its faith which harmonize with America's constitutional order. There is no reason evangelicals and other Christians could not make the same choice on the basis of their own theology. I am asking evangelicals to emulate what the Church of Jesus Christ of Latter-day Saints *does,* not what it *believes.*

Fourth, you can't beat something with nothing. The Church of Fear is more pagan than Christian; it wins its adherents by exploiting some of the darkest elements of human psychology; but it is emotionally compelling and widely present—in politics, in conservative and Christian media, and in the pews. Pastors, understandably bewildered by it, may prefer to ask parishioners to turn away from social media and toward the Bible, but the Church of Jesus Christ of Latter-day Saints shows that more is needed: an emotionally positive, doctrinally coherent, institutionally promoted civic theology which models a Christlike way to do politics.

The church is not monolithic. Some Latter-day Saints

hanker for a sharp-edged, aggressive cultural tone while others pray for a relaxation of conservative strictures on homosexuality and other cultural matters. Yet if I had a dollar for every time a church member, high or low, mentioned the doctrine of agency and the importance of free conscience, I could have just about paid my plane fare to Utah. This doctrinal grounding matters. Among other things, it helps explain why Latter-day Saints, for all their demographic and ideological similarity to white evangelicals, have taken a dimmer view of Trump. (According to data from national exit polls, Latter-day Saints and white evangelicals voted overwhelmingly and in lockstep for the Republican presidential candidates in 2004, 2008, and 2012; but then they diverged, with the Latter-day Saints' support for Trump falling 20 points below white evangelicals' support in 2016, and nine points below in 2020. A poll in 2023 showed that fewer than half of church members approved of him, versus two-thirds of white evangelicals.*)

I am not saying—I hope this is clear—that the measure of a civic theology is whether it impels people to support or oppose a particular person or party. Rather, I am making a broader point: theology matters. Doctrine matters. Like it or not, Christian nationalism and the Church of Fear promote a strong message which today saturates conservative evangelical culture. One pastor summarized it this way: *We need to fight, we need to win.* Pushing back requires a more compelling story—and a more Christian story.

In August 2023, the *New York Times* quoted Representative Brian Mast, a Republican from Florida, as saying: "I want

---

* Daniel A. Cox, "Mormons and White Evangelicals Are Divided over Trump," American Enterprise Institute, December 3, 2019; Samuel Benson, "Will Trump Have a Latter-day Saint Voter Problem Yet Again?" *Deseret News,* September 7, 2023.

my president to be the biggest American chest thumper out there. If you cross him, he will slit your throat, and I get that out of President Trump." I don't know Mr. Mast's religious leanings (though news reports said he had attended an evangelical church), but I do know that a proper Christian civic theology— something Jesus might recognize—would help inoculate us all against bloodthirsty rhetoric and gladiatorial politics.

Tear Down That Wall!

Now for the part authors hate and readers fear (or is it the other way around?): the "what is to be done?" part. I approach that question gingerly and humbly, knowing that Christians may not be eager to hear how an atheistic homosexual Jew thinks they should practice their faith. Fortunately, new paths for Christianity are being mapped and explored by the people whose voices really matter on this question—Christians.

Before we go there, a quick review of where we've been.

First, American Christianity is in crisis. Both of its major streams, the ecumenical and the evangelical, have "thinned," that is, secularized, albeit in very different ways. Neither is as capable of providing meaning and moral grounding as it once was or today needs to be, and secular alternatives like science and SoulCycle cannot, even in principle, fill the void.

Second, like it or not, Christianity's crisis is democracy's crisis, too. Even in our secular, liberal society, Christianity is a load-bearing wall; its failure places dangerous stress on democratic institutions.

Third, despite the claims of post-liberals, Christianity's crisis was not an inevitable result of liberal hyper-individualism or secular cultural aggression; it has been driven primarily by tragic choices made by Christians themselves. Many church members erected a wall of separation between the values they champion in their private lives and the values they express in politics, and they allowed themselves to be seduced by a politicized and un-Christlike Church of Fear.

Fourth, because core Christian principles track closely with core liberal principles, they can be brought into alignment in ways which strengthen both. The Church of Jesus Christ of Latter-day Saints is proving right now, in the real world, that a conservative church can embrace practical pluralism as spiritually exalted and scripturally sound, without watering down the church's doctrine or distinctiveness.

So where does that leave us? What *is* to be done?

Unfortunately, as hard as this is for a Brookings Institution policy wonk to admit, moving Christianity to a healthier place is not in the realm of six-point policy programs. It is in the realm of Christian revival and spiritual formation. As more than one interviewee told me, working to change political behavior is important, but it only treats symptoms. Political dysfunction is a manifestation of the need for civic *discipleship,* the work of aligning hearts more closely with Christ in the public realm. That work requires at least two elements: teaching by pastors, and a civic theology they can teach.

However diminished their authority in the age of cable news and conflict entrepreneurs, pastors remain in every way the point of the evangelical spear. Many are dismayed by the direction their most politicized congregants have taken. But they have been unsure what to do about it. For one thing, their jobs are often insecure. They cannot afford to drive away congregants or split their churches, so they need to tread carefully. For another, they are justifiably reluctant to risk dividing their congregations even further by addressing politics from the pulpit. Many hope, instead, to wait out the Church of Fear. Perhaps the political environment will change, certain divisive politicians will pass from the scene, and radicalized congregants will

grow weary of carrying the culture wars into church and email-
bombing their pastors every Monday morning. Andrew Hanauer,
the founder of the One America Movement, an evangelical
group devoted to reducing toxic polarization in churches and
society, told me, "There's hope among pastors that this nightmare of the last four or five years may lead the church to be
leaner and more of an underdog, which is what it was when it
was born, and less of an entity that's focused on holding on to
political power."

Finally, civic theology—at least of any Madisonian stripe—
has not figured strongly in seminary teaching and pastoral
training. Pastors know what to say about faith, grief, love, and
charity. But what should they say about the comment made by
Donald Trump, Jr., that "turning the other cheek has gotten us
nothing"? Or Simon Kennedy's "The church needs to face this
hard truth: the world has shifted and therefore the age of conciliatory cultural engagement is over. No longer will being nice
and relevant cut it"? Or Ron DeSantis's "And on the eighth day,
God looked down on his planned paradise and said, 'I need a
protector.' So God made a fighter"? Here the doctrine is not so
clear.

The good news I can bring is that the crisis of the Trump
era has brought a widening recognition among Christians that
waiting and hoping and perhaps even praying are not enough.
They see that the wall of separation between personal and civic
spiritual formation must come down, and that the task of dem-
olition requires a new kind of discipleship. "You can't say, 'I'm
a gentle person except when I'm involved in politics,'" as Michael Wear, the president and founder of the new Center for
Christianity and Public Life, put it to me.

Wear has a distinguished career as an evangelical con-
sultant, author, and adviser to politicians (including President
Obama). His new center represents something of a departure,

an effort to address the spiritual formation crisis directly. He described two streams of work, one providing education and fellowships to Christian professionals and civic leaders, the other framing arguments and ideas to spark the public imagination. Hanauer's group, the One America Movement, educates pastors on how to reduce toxic polarization in their churches and connects them with each other so they will feel less isolated or overwhelmed. It gathers pastors for workshops, retreats, and Zoom events; explains the science and theology of polarization; and provides videos, youth-group curricula, and sermon ideas.

Another effort, called The After Party and founded by Curtis Chang, David French, and Russell Moore, seeks to plug the civic-theology gap directly, by equipping pastors and congregational study groups with a scripturally based alternative to the Church of Fear. The After Party's video curriculum, according to its website, "does the complex—but absolutely necessary—theological work of reframing Christian political identity from today's divisive partisan options. Whereas the partisan identity defines political engagement in the 'what' of ideologies, policies, parties, and politicians, The After Party redefines Christian politics around a biblical emphasis on the 'how' of virtues like mercy, humility, and justice."

There are other, similar efforts. How much influence they will have is an open question. Yet the people driving these programs are prominent (if in some cases controversial) voices in the evangelical world, and they reflect a need pastors expressed to me again and again. Just ending the deer-in-the-headlights situation for pastors—when, as Chang put it, "they just hear from the most extreme members of their congregations, so they remain silent and try to white-knuckle through political seasons"—would constitute an important step.

Whatever the fate of The After Party as a particular proj-

ect, the thinking behind it is a good example of how a constructive Christian civic theology might take shape; indeed, already
is taking shape. Chang, a former pulpit pastor now affiliated
with Duke Divinity School and Fuller Theological Seminary,
took me through the logic.

Several years ago, he said, he had come to worry that the
larger culture's hyper-individualism had seeped into the evangelical world. The church had slipped "into a very utilitarian
view of institutions, that they're meant to give us what we need
or want, and if they don't, they're broken. I thought that was
deeply problematic for a number of reasons." One reason made
itself evident on January 6, 2021. "I watched that on TV aghast,"
he said. He was struck not just by the rioters' displays of Christian symbolism but by "the hyper-instrumental view that these
Christians storming the Capitol had of Congress: it wasn't giving us what we want, so we'll just throw it out like a broken
tool. I believe the Bible contains a narrative in which human
institutions are also made in the image of God; institutions are
simply humans in the collective form, mirroring the image of
God. In their own way institutions are human, in a collective
sense, and so in their own way deserve dignity, worth, and intrinsic value."

On January 6, another thought occurred to him: *Where
are the Christian adults to take care of our foundational institutions?* The nihilistic mayhem suggested they "have either been
asleep on the watch and have allowed the foundations to crack
and crumble, or they have actually wielded the wrecking ball.
I could no longer assume there were adults who were going
to take care of these big foundational issues." The narrative of
care and grace which the church preaches toward individuals
"completely goes out the window" where institutions are concerned. "We have no narrative that makes sense of flawed, broken, sinful institutions, so we just treat them as evil." Without

grace toward institutions and a story of how they can be improved and redeemed, nihilism, cynicism, and chaos are only a short step away—as January 6 made clear.

And how to cultivate an ethos of care and stewardship for civic institutions? Begin in churches, Chang told me, because they are the home of evangelicalism and the far right is actively recruiting there. In 2016, MAGA's appeal to evangelicals came as a shock, but "in 2020, there was practically nothing done to equip local churches to have a different approach to politics that was more Jesus-centered. The individual pastors are left to themselves, and they're paralyzed, because they're not equipped." The After Party seeks to fill that gap by developing and teaching a Christlike civic theology.

The reasoning Chang follows to connect personal spiritual formation to civic spiritual formation—to connect Christian ideals with politics and public institutions—is not the same as the theology used by the Church of Jesus Christ of Latter-day Saints; but a family resemblance is not hard to see. Both proffer Christian accounts of why God wants us to care for each other lovingly in the civic sphere, not just the personal sphere; both reject the ethos of permanent warfare, perpetual fear, and us-versus-them; both charge Christians, *as* Christians, with stewardship of the Constitution and its core values of sharing the country and being peacemakers.

If there is to be a rapprochement between the attitudes of white evangelicalism and the institutions of liberal democracy, it will need to be along those lines. And notice: whether paths away from the Church of Fear and toward a Christlike civic theology take the route suggested by Curtis Chang, the route suggested by the Church of Jesus Christ of Latter-day Saints, or some other route altogether, the result will not be to make Christianity more secular, more thin, more sharp. It will be to make Christianity more like itself.

Lessons for Liberals

I need to recognize, before closing, a lacuna in my argument. Having presumptuously scolded Christians for failing to uphold their side of the bargain with liberal democracy, I have yet to say what secular liberals need to do to uphold our side of the deal. The answer is: *more*. I don't think secularism is primarily responsible for Christianity's infirmities; but I do think it could and should be more helpful within the confines of the Constitution's commitment not to promote religion.

As I said in the last chapter, the charge that America is legally or governmentally hostile to Christianity is inaccurate. The current Supreme Court is the friendliest to religion in history. It zealously protects religious prerogatives to hire clergy without interference, to receive government dollars without strings, to preserve freedom of conscience in commercial interactions, even to spend taxpayer dollars at religious schools— something earlier courts balked at. The Religious Freedom Restoration Act, which requires the law to keep well clear of unnecessary impositions on religious belief and practice, stands strong more than 30 years after its nearly unanimous passage. The Respect for Marriage Act, which I discussed earlier, represents a further landmark. In it, Congress—with unanimous Democratic support—prohibited any use of federal dollars and contracts to coerce recognition of same-sex marriage, and it wrote into law the proposition that traditional and religious views of marriage "are held by reasonable and sincere people based on decent and honorable religious or philosophical premises." In other words, the nation's supreme political body definitively repudiated the view, held by many secular progressives, that religious opposition to same-sex marriage should be treated like racial discrimination. Though the Respect for Marriage Act was mostly lost in the news shuffle at the time, it represented a historic de-escalation in the culture war, entirely in the spirit of Madisonian accommodation. No doubt some religious conservatives would prefer even stronger carve-outs. But it is fair to say that in the legal and political realms, American democracy is keeping its founding promise of religious freedom at least as well as it ever has.

In the realm of culture, however, things are less clear. Public confidence in organized religion, as for other institutions, has fallen sharply. Cultural institutions in media and education, while perhaps friendlier to religious worldviews than a generation ago, still struggle to include and understand Christians. The alliances which progressive activists and ecumenical Christians formed in the 1950s and 1960s on issues like civil rights and poverty have attenuated; today's progressives, with their often rigid and sometimes intolerant views on abortion, sexuality, gender, and social justice, have too often let their attitudes toward Christianity be defined by fear of conservative evangelicals. One Democratic presidential administration after another has proved tone-deaf to religious concerns. In a depressingly recurrent pattern, Democratic White Houses promise to cultivate faith-based constituencies but then ignore, marginalize, or sacrifice them. Christian friends of mine who have worked inside Democratic administrations say the problem has less to do with animus than obliviousness; most politically active Democrats, especially younger ones, grew up in secular families and have secular friends and secular educations. They may mean no harm to Christianity, but they lack the vocabulary and intellectual equipment to receive religious wavelengths.

Liberal ideology, too, has drifted toward rigid church-state separation—not just legally but culturally and attitudinally. The major "wall of separation" decisions of the Warren and Burger courts instilled the idea that any mixing of government and religion is intolerable. While the current Supreme Court has (rightly, in my view) pulled back from separatist absolutism, a cultural residue of intolerance persists. As someone who has been persecuted in the name of Jesus Christ because of my sexual orientation, I understand where Americans United for Separation of Church and State and the Freedom From Religion Foundation are coming from; I am against religious establishment. The government should not officially prefer any particular religion, or prefer religiosity over non-religiosity. I don't think a public school should open the day with a prayer even if the prayer is nondenominational, because I know from experience how uncomfortable and excluded this makes unbelieving and minority students feel. The country is rapidly diversifying along religious as well as other lines, and calls by post-liberals for the government to throw a life preserver to Christianity are as outdated as they are impractical.

Yet efforts by secular groups and activists to police the landscape for religious incursions into the public sector seem to me equally misguided and counterproductive. Too often, my secular friends are inclined to regard faith-based concerns as trivial, superstitious, or bigoted. While I see the Bible as human-created and therefore flawed, it is a foundation of American moral culture and will remain so; it should be taught as foundational and treated with respect, even when criticized. I believe the reading of scripture as condemning loving, committed homosexual relationships is hermeneutically and morally mistaken, for reasons well explained by people like Matthew Vines and James Brownson; but I do recognize that a sincere reading of scripture, even a sincere *mis*reading, is not necessarily the same thing as homophobia and can be accompanied by goodwill. When I encounter Christians who disapprove of my homosexuality but mean me no harm and aren't hypocritical, I try to respond with persuasion, not condemnation. And although I regard supernaturalism as no basis for moral claims, that does not entail rejecting the Bible as a source of moral teaching. I have heard sermons, Christian and Jewish, whose exacting biblical exegesis left me feeling closer to truth. Too often, secular Americans have acted as if allergic to religious teaching. We should never, ever, pass a law because someone thinks Jesus said to; yet our laws might be better if we more often asked what Jesus might have said about them.

And too many secular Americans, perhaps through ignorance of religion and American history, see accommodating faith as a zero-sum game in which religion's gain is equality's loss. They seem unaware that religious freedom is *the* founding principle of the United States; that the First Amendment specifically carves out religious observance as a distinct and privileged category, not just as one of many competing claims; that our laws (including the landmark civil rights laws of the 1960s) have long included religious accommodations and exemptions, usually without controversy. When my LGBT friends demand that their weddings be served by *every* business, no matter the enterprise's size, location, or faith, they may see enforcement of customers' civil rights, but I see doctrinaire totalism. If a balance can be struck allowing the large majority of LGBT couples to obtain wedding services while exempting a modest number of mostly small businesses, that is not a win for one side and a loss for the other; it is a win for both, because it de-escalates the tensions which tear the fabric of pluralism. In that respect, the LGBT community, and secular Americans generally, have a lot to learn from the Church of Jesus Christ of Latter-day Saints. In a diverse country full of moral disagreement, a disposition toward "patience, negotiation, and mutual accommodation" is a win-win proposition.

How might the country be different, I wonder, if more students from secular backgrounds were exposed to comparative religion courses which respectfully examined the Bible and its sources alongside other religious traditions? How much might the culture wars be pacified if secular liberals were eager rather than reluctant to find accommodations with faith-based communities? How much more truly inclusive would workplaces and universities be if people of faith were routinely included in diversity and inclusion efforts, and if anti-religious bigotry were rejected as firmly as other biases? How much better informed might news coverage and other media products be if religious perspectives were reliably sought out and knowledgeably covered, and if newsrooms included more reporters who were openly devout? How much better informed might unbelievers be if we cultivated Christian friends, approached their faith with open-hearted curiosity, and perhaps now and then accompanied them to church? And how much deeper and truer would liberalism itself be if secular liberals more fully recognized how much our democracy leans on faith traditions?

You, reader, are as good a judge as I. My own thought for liberals, however, is that it is not enough to be tolerant or accepting of religion. We should be *welcoming*. We should even, perhaps, *cherish* religion.

I am not saying we liberals should endorse a religion or uncritically embrace its teachings. (Very few openly gay people or atheists would say that!) I am saying there is a great deal in faith traditions, emphatically including Christianity, which we can admire; and when we disagree with a faith tradition, we should do so respectfully and give it a second or even third hearing; and when we criticize faith, we should do so in a spirit of humility, recognizing that the great faith traditions have been around a lot longer than liberalism.

And we should remember that, however transformative liberalism has been as an engine of economic, scientific, and social advancement, it is not self-sufficient. We secular liberals can't make it on our own. We must do what we can to help our religious friends help us.

Make Christianity Peculiar Again

When worried evangelicals talk about the politicization and paganization of the church, they naturally express frustration and dismay. Yet some of them, such as Karen Swallow Prior and Russell Moore, also express hope. "We're in a place of disruption and loss," Moore said in a 2023 podcast interview with the journalist Jon Ward. "That is always the way God works in terms of creating something new. The primary thing is to say to people, don't panic about the sense of homelessness that you feel. Don't panic about the kind of bewilderment that you feel. That actually can be a sign of grace."*

In another 2023 interview, with the podcaster Charlie Sykes, Moore rejected the idea that the church can solve its crisis by returning to the status quo ante.

> Instead, I think what you have happening is people who really didn't know they were on the same team are realizing they are. New kinds of collaborations are coming out of that in church planning movements, mission strategies, and all kinds of ways. So it's not going to be the same kind of cohesive movement; it's going to be different. But in history, that's always how it happens. John and Charles Wesley don't take over the Church of England, they step out and start something new. And I don't think we're

* Jon Ward, "How Russell Moore Learned to Stop Worrying and Embrace the Apocalypse," July 21, 2023, available at toppodcast.com/podcast_feeds /the-long-game/.

going to have a big battle for the soul of evangelicalism
and somebody's going to win and somebody's going to
lose. I think instead you just have a splintering.*

Out of that splintering, he said, will come seeds of regenera-
tion. Perhaps it is not too much to hope that new ways to connect Christianity and democracy will arise.

To fertilize the soil for that sort of change, one element of
spiritual formation seems especially important—a mindset
which I can claim, as a trifecta minority, to understand. One
finds it among Jews, homosexuals, and atheists as well as within
the Church of Jesus Christ of Latter-day Saints. Christians sometimes call it an *exilic* mindset. I might call it *minoritarian*.

Now, white evangelicals are well aware that, as Robert P.
Jones puts it in his book *The End of White Christian America*,
"White Christian America's heyday has passed." They know
that the white Protestant population is aging and not being
replenished, that white evangelicals' share of the population
has dropped sharply, and that only a miracle could turn things
around. In that sense, they are keenly aware of minority status.
The open question, a question on which the outlook for American democracy depends, is how they adjust: whether they hun-
ker down within the Church of Fear, nursing grievances and
a sense of embattlement and betrayal—or, as Jon Ward writes
in his 2023 book *Testimony*, they instead become "a Christian
community that lays down its love of dominance and getting
its own way and embraces the idea of being a minority. . . .
That kind of thinking would make conservative white evangelicals much better neighbors."

In a visionary lecture at Fuller Theological Seminary in

---

* Charlie Sykes, "Russell Moore: 'Losing Our Religion,'" *The Bulwark,* July
28, 2023.

2017, Mark Labberton, then the seminary's president, explained that Christianity is a religion of exile, not dominion. Christianity is intended to be peculiar, not ordinary; countercultural, not consumerist. "The church would be more faithful, more distinctly Christ's people, if we actually understood that we don't live in the promised land; we live in exile," he said. Instead, "what seems to define a great deal of the American church is fear. . . . What if the crisis of this moment is actually a deep invitation to a new way of understanding our location? Our identity? Our living, breathing experiences of what this can mean?" He continued: "Today may we be faithful exiles. For it's that that will reveal the reality of the love of God who knows and sees people in exile, to restore and remake them to be the light and salt that can do as exiles what only we can do."*

I understand how challenging the exilic mindset can be. In the 1980s, gay people watched many Christian congregations turn their backs on AIDS patients, some even saying God sent the plague to punish us. There has never been a safer, more welcoming country for Jews, yet even in the United States we have seen mass murder at a synagogue and parades of menacing men chanting "Jews will not replace us!"—and then, in street rallies and on college campuses after Hamas went to war with Israel, chants of "From the river to the sea!" Although neo-Nazis are thankfully fringe elements, Jews still grow up with a sense of being outsiders looking in. We always will.

I treasure feeling like an outsider, although the exilic mindset is admittedly an acquired taste. If you offered to let me rerun my life as a heterosexual white Protestant who saw my values reflected all around me and never needed to think about being persecuted or stigmatized, I would reject the deal.

* Labberton's talk can be viewed at www.youtube.com/watch?v=HGUf5 cuRWoU.

Injustice is only visible from society's margin, and doing what I can to contend against it has been my life's greatest privilege. I can testify that the exilic life, while sometimes frustrating or challenging or dangerous, is a blessing, not a curse; a source of redemption more than oppression; a call to humility and compassion.

Can conservative white Protestantism make its peace with exilic life? Can it realign with America's liberal tradition? I think so; I hope so. I take hope from Russell Moore's comment, in his interview with Ward, that every Christian gets a vote. "I don't think," he said, "that those big, market-driven, entrepreneurial measures, which really led us into this crisis, are going to get us out of it. You can't fix the movement, whatever that is. You can't fix the church. You can't fix the country. But what you can do is dissent in ways of saying, 'I don't have to conform myself to that.' And when you have small groups of people who can see and can model a different way, that's how every change happens that's meaningful."

In researching this book, I met many Christians who have modeled a different, countercultural, *peculiar* way. One of them is Rusty Bowers, the former Arizona House speaker. Though he is a conservative Republican, he stood up against MAGA's effort to reverse the 2020 election in Arizona. Under intense pressure from then-President Trump and Trump's lawyer and henchman Rudy Giuliani, he told them, "You are asking me to do something against my oath and I will not break my oath." Then he testified bravely before the January 6 Committee on Capitol Hill; his reward was to be censured by the state Republican Party and defeated in a state Senate primary.

I cannot do better than to quote the last words of my interview with him. As our conversation closed, I asked how he was keeping busy after politics. He replied that he was working on an initiative to encourage compromise and civility, "and then a resurgence of patriotism. I do believe there's faith, and I do believe there's hope. And without hope, there is nothing; there is rapid decline. We choose to have hope to make faith work."

EPILOGUE
A Parting Message

Dear Mark—

After college, we drifted apart. You married Anne, your college sweetheart, became one of the world's leading scholars of mystical Christianity, fathered two children. I came out as gay, built a career in journalism, threw myself into the cause of same-sex marriage, and found a husband. We vaguely kept track of one another and saw each other at college reunions. In photos, you aged not at all: still tall and broad and the picture of health. I assumed we could always catch up later, as one does.

One day I received an email from Anne. Did I know you had ALS?

My heart sank to a dark place. I knew too much about amyotrophic lateral sclerosis, commonly called Lou Gehrig's disease. My father had died of a neurological ailment, one which, like ALS, rendered his body a shell and did not respond to treatment. That such a fate would befall you, of all people, seemed like an act of heavenly spite.

During the pandemic, we connected on Zoom. Then, when travel reopened, I and a mutual college friend traveled to Chicago. Anne greeted us and showed us to the garden in back of the house. It was a place of flowers and bees, dazzling and colorful on a sunny autumn day, incongruously bright amid the gloom of our mission. I confess I was afraid of what I might encounter. But we did not find a bitter or angry or depressed man.

You were wheelchair bound, unable to move your body, drawing oxygen through a straw slung over your shoulder, attended by a full-time aide. Thank goodness, you had been spared, so far, the final stage of ALS, the inability to speak and communicate, the dreaded condition of being locked in. You were even finishing a book, thanks to dictation software and graduate students, and had another in the pipeline.

You told us you had researched assorted diseases and concluded that, among all of them, ALS was the one you least wanted to have. And yet your tone was wry, not harsh. Even in extremis, your faith seemed undiminished. I think that was the moment when, in all my life, I most acutely felt my own shallowness and spiritual poverty. I cannot understand why, if there is a God, he sends such terrible scourges to afflict his most devoted servants. But seeing your lack of anger, I tried to shelve my own. I saw how your trust in God gave you courage and grace amid an unbearable ordeal. That was, to me, a more powerful witness on behalf of the Christian faith than any words or argument could have borne.

You tired quickly; speech was a struggle; we left after an hour so as not to wear you out. I departed fearing what would come next, a fear you shared. You knew that ALS was coming for your power of speech, that you would be silenced and shut in, unable to write and communicate; you hoped nature would take its course before that happened.

Only a few weeks later, I received word from Anne. After lunch, you had retired to read and passed peacefully. You got your wish, a mercy you had more than earned.

I don't believe in an afterlife or eternal soul. That solace is not available to me. Still, Tim Keller once told me that God hears the prayers of atheists. If that's the case, I pray you're reading this.

But Georg Solti and the Chicago Symphony brass *were* overrated.

Notes on Sources

A small book on a big topic necessarily stands on the shoulders of giants. I could not have written this volume without drawing upon the work of many insightful scholars, journalists, and experts. In general, I have cited key sources in the text. Here I provide more detail on works consulted.

Liberalism and its critics. Three classic texts have framed my understanding of the debate about modern liberalism. One is Alasdair MacIntyre's *After Virtue: A Study in Moral Theory* (Notre Dame, 1981; third edition 2007), which accuses post-Enlightenment individualism of fostering moral disarray. A second is George F. Will's *Statecraft as Soulcraft: What Government Does* (Simon & Schuster, 1984), which argues that liberal government necessarily molds morals and cannot coherently claim neutrality. In response to those and other arguments, William Galston's *Liberal Purposes: Goods, Virtues, and Diversity in the Liberal State* (Cambridge, 1991) argues compellingly that liberalism properly understood is neither neutral nor "thin" but value-rich and morally demanding (even if liberals themselves often fail to notice this).

Among today's conservative critics of liberalism, several prominent theorists assert that liberalism is self-undermining and must be supplanted or at least supplemented by governance based on religiously grounded "common good" principles. Patrick J. Deneen's case is in *Why Liberalism Failed* (Yale, 2018) and *Regime Change: Toward a Postliberal Future* (Sentinel, 2023). Adrian Vermeule, who, like Deneen, brings a Catholic perspective, argues for "common-good constitutionalism" in an article in *The Atlantic*, "Beyond Originalism" (March 31, 2020). Yoram Hazony brings a non-Christian (but pro-Christian) perspective on post-liberalism in *Conservatism: A Rediscovery* (Regnery, 2022). For historical context on theoretical challenges to liberalism from the right, see Matthew Rose, *A World After Liberalism: Five Thinkers Who Inspired the Radical Right* (Yale, 2021). Simon McCarthy-Jones's *Freethinking: Protecting Freedom of Thought Amidst the New Battle for the Mind* (Oneworld, 2023) contains an astute encapsulation and analysis of the post-liberal viewpoint.

Thoughtful rejoinders to post-liberalism defend liberalism while recognizing its imperfections and considering ways to improve it. Francis Fukuyama's compact yet ambitious *Liberalism and Its Discontents* (Farrar, Straus and Giroux, 2022) makes a good point of entry. I draw on various articles by the liberal theorist Peter Berkowitz, notably his five-part series "Anti-Liberal Zealotry" in the online publication *RealClear Policy* (September 14–28, 2018). Berkowitz's review of Hazony's book, "Redefining Conservatism to Remake America," in the online *Washington Free Beacon* (May 29, 2022), is similarly compelling. In his Substack blog *The Permanent Problem*, Brink Lindsey examines the crises of liberalism, capitalism, and modernity, thinking in refreshingly creative directions. Michael Walzer summarizes his critique of post-liberalism in his conversation with Yascha Mounk for the online journal *Persuasion* ("Michael Walzer on Liberalism and Its Critics," July 8, 2023; available on YouTube), further elaborated in his article "Notes on a Dangerous Mistake" in *Liberties* journal (Winter

2024). David Corey, in his meticulously argued review of Deneen's *Why Liberalism Failed,* shows how post-liberalism's overbroad claims undercut its sometimes astute observations ("Against the Deformations of Liberalism," *American Affairs,* undated, americanaffairsjournal.org/2018/02/against-the-defor mations-of-liberalism).

Christianity and secularism. Science has a lot to say about the development and sociology of religion; for a panoramic overview, see Robert Wright's *The Evolution of God* (Little, Brown, 2009). Christian Smith provides a valuable account of religion's distinguishing characteristics and functions in *Religion: What It Is, How It Works, and Why It Matters* (Princeton, 2017). Hugh Heclo's *Christianity and American Democracy* (Harvard, 2007) approaches classic status on its titular subject. A book which deserves to attain classic status is Robert Tracy McKenzie's *We the Fallen People: The Founders and the Future of American Democracy* (InterVarsity, 2021), a bracing critique of America's abandonment of the Founders' Christianity-inflected realism about human nature. An account of populism's influence on American Christianity is Nathan O. Hatch's *The Democratization of American Christianity* (Yale, 1989).

The turn toward secularism within the United States and abroad has received much attention. For a theorized analysis of the (literal) disenchantment which has followed from secularism, Charles Taylor's *A Secular Age* (Harvard, 2007) is a touchstone, if anything more relevant today than when first published. Also seminal is Joseph Bottum's *An Anxious Age: The Post-Protestant Ethic and the Spirit of America* (Random House, 2014), which argues that the decline of mainline Protestantism has discombobulated America's politics and culture. Ross Douthat explores similar themes, and foretells today's dysfunctions, in *Bad Religion: How We Became a Nation of Heretics* (Free Press, 2012). More optimistic about the durability and

health of Christianity, and religion in general, are Robert D.
Putnam and David E. Campbell's *American Grace: How Religion Divides and Unites Us* (Simon & Schuster, 2010) and John
Micklethwait and Adrian Wooldridge's *God Is Back: How the
Global Revival of Faith Is Changing the World* (Penguin, 2009).
Both are somewhat dated but still repay attention.

Religious trends and practices. For statistical profiles of
religious belief and practice, copious research published by the
Public Religion Research Institute, such as the regular Census
of American Religion, is indispensable. The same is true of
opinion research by the Pew Research Center, available online
at the center's "religion" topic page. Ryan Burge, in his Substack blog *Graphs About Religion,* provides detailed statistical
analysis of trends. Among narrative analyses of the decline of
Christian observance and the rise of ex-Christians and "nones"
(Americans who are not affiliated with any organized religion)
are Robert P. Jones's *The End of White Christian America* (Simon
& Schuster, 2016); Stephen Bullivant's *Nonverts: The Making of
Ex-Christian America* (Oxford, 2022); and Jim Davis and Michael Graham's *The Great Dechurching: Who's Leaving, Why Are
They Going, and What Will It Take to Bring Them Back?* (with
Ryan P. Burge; Zondervan, 2023). Bob Smietana's *Reorganized
Religion: The Reshaping of the American Church and Why It
Matters* (Worthy Books, 2022) focuses on change at the congregational level, especially the downsizing of Protestant churches.

Evidence has accumulated that religious participation is
healthy for individuals and communities, and that the decline
in religious participation may have harmful effects. Useful accounts are found in Tyler J. VanderWeele, "Religion and Health:
A Synthesis," from M. J. Balboni and J. R. Peteet, eds., *Spirituality and Religion within the Culture of Medicine: From Evidence
to Practice* (Oxford, 2017); and Tyler Giles, Daniel M. Hungerman, and Tamar Oostrom, "Opiates of the Masses? Deaths of

Despair and the Decline of American Religion" (National Bureau of Economic Research, January 2023). Challenging the notion that choosing a faith is a matter of convenience like shopping, Laurence R. Iannaccone shows that stricter, more demanding forms of religious observance provide more personal and social value ("Why Strict Churches Are Strong," *American Journal of Sociology,* March 1994, and "Introduction to the Economics of Religion," *Journal of Economic Literature,* September 1998). Tara Isabella Burton's richly reported *Strange Rites: New Religions for a Godless World* (PublicAffairs, 2020) demonstrates that secular pseudo-religions and personal-development movements are poor substitutes for more traditional forms of religious observance.

White evangelicalism in the United States. The term "evangelical"—indeed, the concept itself—is capacious and often confusing. Thomas S. Kidd's *Who Is an Evangelical? The History of a Movement in Crisis* (Yale, 2019) is a good brief introduction to the movement from the first Great Awakening to the Trump era. For a deeply reported narrative history, see Frances FitzGerald's *The Evangelicals: The Struggle to Shape America* (Simon & Schuster, 2017). In his 2023 book *The Kingdom, the Power, and the Glory: American Evangelicals in an Age of Extremism,* Tim Alberta combines reporting with personal history to paint a sympathetic yet worried (and worrying) account of contemporary white evangelicalism (HarperCollins). From an evangelical viewpoint, the Barna Group and Alpha USA provide insights and data in *Reviving Evangelicalism: Current Realities That Demand a New Vision for Sharing Faith* (Barna, 2019).

Not being Christian, much less evangelical, I lean on analysts and critics of white evangelicalism who are in, or at least of, the movement. The voluminous writings and interviews of Russell Moore provide essential inspiration for this book. I have

drawn on an assortment of his articles and podcasts, as cited
in the main text, plus his book *Losing Our Religion: An Altar
Call for Evangelical America* (Sentinel, 2023). Moore's criticisms
of the movement, while sometimes scorching, come from a
place of love. The same is true of columns and interviews by
David French, which have appeared in the *New York Times,
The Dispatch,* and other outlets—and which, like Moore's work,
have provided indispensable guidance. In *Christianity's American Fate: How Religion Became More Conservative and Society
More Secular* (Princeton, 2022), David A. Hollinger recounts
how white evangelicalism and Republican partisanship ex-
changed their DNA. In *Jesus and John Wayne: How White
Evangelicals Corrupted a Faith and Fractured a Nation* (W.W.
Norton, 2020), Kristin Kobes Du Mez argues that gender tra-
ditionalism and an ethos of "militant masculinity" redefined
the movement. No discussion of evangelicalism's evangelical
critics is complete without mention of Mark A. Noll's bomb-
shell 1994 book *The Scandal of the Evangelical Mind* (Eerdmans,
republished with new material in 2022). For more-personal accounts of crisis in the white evangelical world, see Jon Ward's
*Testimony: Inside the Evangelical Movement That Failed a Gen-
eration* (Brazos, 2023) and Christine Rosen's *My Fundamental-
ist Education: A Memoir of a Divine Girlhood* (PublicAffairs,
2005). Both memoirs are intimate, conscientious, and sometimes anguished.

Christian nationalism. Although the phenomenon of
Christian nationalism is difficult to pin down, considerable
polling and analysis have deepened scholarly understanding.
Perhaps the most comprehensive opinion research comes from
the Public Religion Research Institute, notably its 2023 *American Values Survey* and its report *A Christian Nation? Understanding the Threat of Christian Nationalism to American Democracy and Culture* (February 8, 2023). Several books have

defined and examined the phenomenon from both U.S. and international perspectives. In *The Godless Crusade: Religion, Populism and Right-Wing Identity Politics in the West* (Cambridge, 2023), Tobias Cremer observes Christian nationalism in France, Germany, and the United States and finds that it is a secular, not religious, movement. Philip S. Gorski and Samuel L. Perry reach the same conclusion in *The Flag + the Cross: White Christian Nationalism and the Threat to American Democracy* (Oxford, 2022)—as does Rogers Brubaker in his 2017 article "Between Nationalism and Civilizationism: The European Populist Moment in Comparative Perspective" (in *Ethnic and Racial Studies* 40:8).

Many analysts agree that Christian nationalism, at least in its more potent forms, is inconsistent with liberal democracy. Paul D. Miller makes this case in *The Religion of American Greatness: What's Wrong with Christian Nationalism* (InterVarsity, 2022). David P. Gushee defines and unpacks what he calls "authoritarian reactionary Christianity" in *Defending Democracy from Its Christian Enemies* (Eerdmans, 2023). In an interview on Jon Ward's "The Long Game" podcast (February 17, 2023), Matthew D. Taylor provides a disturbing account of the "New Apostolic Reformation" movement and its radicalizing effects (available at toppodcast.com/podcast_feeds/the-long -game/). The Baptist Joint Committee for Religious Liberty, the Freedom From Religion Foundation, and Christians Against Christian Nationalism explore links between Christian supremacists and far-right extremism in their report *Christian Nationalism and the January 6, 2021, Insurrection* (undated; issued February 9, 2022).

The Church of Jesus Christ of Latter-day Saints. A valuable analysis of the church's unique structural and social characteristics is contained in Putnam and Campbell, *American Grace,* cited above. On the church's history, I draw upon Michael J. Lee and R. Jarrod Atchison, *We Are Not One People: Secession and Separatism in American Politics Since 1776* (Oxford, 2022), as well as valuable articles by W. Paul Reeve: "The Council of Fifty and the Search for Religious Liberty," in Matthew J. Grow and R. Eric Smith, eds., *The Council of Fifty: What the Records Reveal about Mormon History* (Brigham Young University, 2017); and "The Mormon Church in Utah," in Terryl L. Givens and Philip L. Barlow, eds., *Oxford Handbook of Mormonism* (Oxford, 2015).

For authoritative accounts of church teaching on agency, choice, and sin, I draw upon Terryl L. Givens's *Wrestling the Angel: The Foundations of Mormon Thought: Cosmos, God, Humanity* (Oxford, 2015), as well as Terryl Givens and Fiona Givens, *The God Who Weeps: How Mormonism Makes Sense of Life* (Ensign Peak, 2012). The speeches and writings of Dallin Oaks of the church's First Presidency (cited in the text) are canonical on the church's understanding of pluralism and make constitutional arguments which are impressive in their own right.

Civic theology. James Alison's richly insightful interview with Andrew Sullivan on the fundamentals of Christianity is available at andrewsullivan.substack.com/p/james-alison-on-christianity. For a thoughtful and soulful perspective on Christlike political engagement, see Michael Wear's *The Spirit of Our Politics: Spiritual Formation and the Renovation of Public Life* (Zondervan, 2024). Years after it was delivered on June 9, 2017, Mark Labberton's address at Fuller Theological Seminary, "Beauty in Exile" (available on YouTube), remains relevant and, indeed, beautiful.

My epigraph is from George Lawrence's translation of Alexis de Tocqueville's *Democracy in America* (volume 1, part 2, chapter 9; ed. J. P. Meyer, Doubleday, 1969).

Index

Adams, John, 19, 20
Ahmari, Sohrab, 11, 46
Alison, James, 69, 82
Augustine (saint), 113
Ayer, A. J., 25

Bakker, Jim, 54
Balmer, Randall, 53
Beatles (music group), 7–8
Berger, Peter, 18
Berkowitz, Peter, 44, 46
Biden, Joe, 87
Bolsonaro, Jair, 76
Bottum, Joseph, 35
Bowers, Rusty, 112–113, 116, 136–137
Brooks, David, 35
Brownson, James, 130
Bullivant, Stephen, 10, 11
Burge, Ryan, 56–58
Burger, Warren, 129
Burton, Tara Isabella, 16–17
Bush, George H. W., 1
Bush, George W., 55, 63

Carter, Jimmy, 55
Catholicism, 49, 60, 69, 101–102,
    109

Center for Christianity and Public
    Life, 124–125
Chang, Curtis, 58, 125–127
Charles, Tommy, 7
Christianity: authoritarian reac-
    tionary, 78; confident, 89; con-
    servative, 10, 11, 15, 48, 50, 58, 81,
    100–101, 104, 119; crisis of, 5–6,
    8, 11, 34–36, 39, 74, 87, 97, 122;
    cultural, 58; decline of, 4–5, 8–11,
    39; democracy and, 5–8, 18–21,
    35–36, 40, 82, 87–90, 97, 134;
    discipleship and, 88, 123, 124;
    ethical norms of, 66; exilic mind-
    set and, 134–135; grace in, 3, 69,
    85–86, 126–127, 133, 139; identifi-
    cation with, 9, 11; LGBT people
    condemned by, 2, 67, 101; liberal-
    ism and, 33, 89, 129; mainline,
    9–11, 19, 52–54, 60, 106, 122, 129;
    morality and, 69, 71; mysticism
    and, 3, 29, 138; negative views
    of, 2, 3; Nietzsche on, 13–14; pil-
    lars of, 69, 82; public vs. private,
    71–72, 88, 119; secular influences
    on, 52–54, 87; sharp, 5, 37–92;
    thick, 6, 93–137; thin, 5, 7–36, 39;

Christianity (*continued*)
  U.S. Constitution and, 89; values
   and, 14, 34, 49, 61, 71–76, 119
Christian nationalism: adherents
  of, 79–82; characteristics of,
  78–79; civic theology and, 94,
  117, 118, 121; as international
  phenomenon, 80–81; Madisonian pluralism and, 116
Church of Jesus Christ of Latter-
  day Saints: agency in, 112–118,
  120, 121; on California Proposition 8 (2008), 99, 120; Church
  of Fear rejected by, 104; civic
  theology of, 93–97, 117–121, 127;
  conservatism of, 100–101, 104;
  Council of Fifty, 110; educational
  programs, 104–105, 107; exilic
  mindset and, 134; expansion
  of, 106; on Fairness for All Act
  (proposed), 100; First Presidency, 93; ministering brothers
  and sisters program, 106; missionary work by, 105; persecution of, 108–109, 111; on religious
  pluralism, 108–111; Romney as
  member of, 55; theology of,
  93–97, 103–104, 112–121, 127; on
  Trump, 121; on U.S. Constitution, 93, 96, 102, 103, 116; on
  Utah SB 296 (2015), 98
Clinton, Bill, 64
Clinton, Hillary, 63, 64
Cox, Spencer, 35–36
Cranney, Stephen, 106
Cremer, Tobias, 80–81

Darwin, Charles, 26
Davis, Jim, 8–9
Dawkins, Richard, 26

Deneen, Patrick, 11, 42–43, 46,
  47–49
DeSantis, Ron, 124
Dionne, E. J., 56
Du Mez, Kristin Kobes, 65–66, 70,
  79, 91
Durkheim, Émile, 26

evangelicalism: authoritarianism
  and, 19; battlefield mindset and,
  37–38; challenges for, 50–51;
  Christian nationalism and,
  79–82; culture wars and, 68,
  70, 124; decline of, 9–11, 106;
  democracy and, 90; exilic
  mindset and, 134; fear and,
  69–70, 121, 129, 134; "Flight 93,"
  37, 83, 117, 119; in Global South,
  51; identifiers of, 9; illiberalism
  and, 120; MAGA movement
  and, 65–67, 73, 127; media influences on, 91; partisanship
  and, 40, 54–59, 61, 68; pastoral
  authority and, 90–91, 123; public
  disapproval of, 60; Religious
  Right and, 58, 81; Republican
  Party and, 54–58, 67, 104; resurgence of, 8; on same-sex marriage, 101–102; secularization
  of, 52, 73–74, 122; spiritual
  formation and, 87–88, 134;
  splintering within, 134; Trump
  and, 58, 61, 63–68, 72–73, 121;
  values of, 59

Faith Communities Today, 9
Faulkner, William, 110
Feynman, Richard, 24
First Amendment, 60, 109, 131
Flake, Kathleen, 112

Forsyth, James, 70
Franklin, Benjamin, 51
French, David, 60, 71–72, 88, 125
Fukuyama, Francis, 44

Galston, William, 44, 56
Garlow, Jim, 75–78
Gerson, Michael, 68, 70
Gilbert, Clark, 104–106
Giuliani, Rudy, 136
Givens, Fiona, 114
Givens, Terryl, 112, 114, 115
Graham, Billy, 55
Graham, Michael, 8–9
Grose, Jessica, 17
Guinness, Os, 64
Gushee, David P., 43, 78

Hamas, 135
Hanauer, Andrew, 87–88, 124, 125
Harris, Sam, 26
Hazony, Yoram, 11
Heclo, Hugh, 20
Hollinger, David A., 34–35, 52, 53, 66, 90
Hudson, Alexandra, 85–86
Hume, David, 26; "Of Miracles," 30–31
Hunter, James Davison, 28

James, William, 4, 24–25
Jay, John, 47
Jefferson, Thomas, 19
Jesus Christ: imitation of, 70–72, 82, 84–86, 90; privatized views of, 88; resurrection of, 30, 31; rivals to fame of, 7–8; teachings of, 6, 39, 69, 72, 85; theological affinity for, 57
Jones, Robert P., 11, 80, 134

Kant, Immanuel, 84
Keller, Tim, 4, 30, 140
Kennedy, Simon, 124
Kidd, Thomas S., 56
King, Martin Luther, Jr., 55

Labberton, Mark, 34, 135
Lennon, John, 7, 9, 10
liberal democracy: Christianity and, 5–6, 8, 40, 82, 90; compromise in, 86, 94; fear and, 83; institutions of, 127; political choices and, 12; secularization and, 32; threats to, 91; triumphalism and, 18
liberalism: achievements of, 47; Christianity and, 33, 89, 129; on church-state separation, 21, 129–130; classical, 12, 107; critiques of, 12–15, 36, 40–49, 107–108, 119; faith and, 41, 42; lessons for, 128–133; Madisonian, 45, 48; mischaracterizations of, 45–47; morality and, 84; neoliberalism, 50; Nietzsche on, 13, 14; pluralism and, 43, 81, 94, 108; U.S. Constitution and, 5, 47; use of term, 11–12; values and, 33–34, 42–44, 48, 82, 85–86, 92; weakening of, 6
Lincoln, Abraham, 85
Lindsey, Brink, 18, 36, 41
Locke, John, 4, 45, 46

Machiavelli, Niccolò, 72
Madison, James, 4, 48, 83, 86, 94–96, 98
MAGA movement: Christian nationalism and, 80; efforts to overturn 2020 election, 136;

MAGA movement (*continued*)
  evangelicals and, 65–67, 73, 127;
  fascist elements of, 87
Margolis, Michele F., 57
Mast, Brian, 121–122
Matzko, Paul, 59, 69
McCain, John, 55, 63
McCarthy-Jones, Simon, 41–42, 45
McIntosh, Anne, 138–139
McIntosh, Mark A., 1–6, 138–140
McWhorter, John, 16
Micklethwait, John, 17, 51
Mohler, Albert, 67
Moore, Russell, 34–36, 58, 68–69,
  72–74, 79, 89, 125, 133–134, 136

Nader, Ralph, 1, 4
Nedelisky, Paul, 28
Nelson, Russell M., 93
Netanyahu, Benjamin, 76
Nietzsche, Friedrich, 13–15, 17, 38,
  50

Oaks, Dallin, 93–96, 102–103, 108,
  111–112, 114–116
Obama, Barack, 64, 124
Orbán, Viktor, 48, 49, 76
Orwell, George, 4

Peirce, C. S., 4
Perry, Samuel L., 79, 80
Peterson, Chris, 36
Plato, 25, 50
Popper, Karl, 4
Prior, Karen Swallow, 133

Reagan, Ronald, 54
Reeve, Paul, 108, 110
Romney, Mitt, 55, 63
Rouse, Stella, 81
Russell, Bertrand, 3, 4

secularism and secularization:
  challenges of, 50–51; Christian
  nationalism and, 80–81; culture
  and, 15, 59, 61, 74; of evangelicalism, 52, 73–74, 122; interdependence with religion,
  21–23, 32–33, 39; liberal democracy and, 32; limitations of,
  15–17, 23, 24, 27; of mainline
  Christianity, 52–54, 122; morality
  and, 15, 25–27, 39; mortality and,
  23, 24, 27; politics and, 5, 15;
  post-liberal views of, 12–13, 40;
  pseudo-religions and, 17; spiritual formation and, 87–88;
  theology and, 52; values and,
  15, 33–34
Smietana, Bob, 10
Smith, Adam, 26, 84
Smith, David Livingstone, 82
Smith, Joseph, 104, 108–111, 115
Solti, Georg, 1, 140
Stuart, Brad, 23–24
Sullivan, Andrew, 69
Sykes, Charlie, 133

Telhami, Shibley, 81
Thomas, Clarence, 100
Thumma, Scott, 9
Tisby, Jemar, 79
Tocqueville, Alexis de, 20, 21
Trump, Donald, 7, 38, 39, 47, 58,
  61–68, 70, 72–73, 80, 83, 121
Trump, Donald, Jr., 71, 124

VanderWeele, Tyler J., 17
Vermeule, Adrian, 11
Vines, Matthew, 130

Walker, Andrew, 101–102
Wallace, George, 55, 66

Walzer, Michael, 49

Ward, Jon, 83, 88, 133, 134, 136

Warren, Earl, 129

Wear, Michael, 88, 90, 124–125

Wehner, Peter, 58, 68, 70

Wesley, John and Charles, 133

Whitehead, Andrew L., 79, 80

Will, George F., 20–21

Williams, Troy, 98–99

Wooldridge, Adrian, 17, 51

Zuckerman, Phil, 17